D. L. Scott-Browne

Scott-Browne's Text-Book of Phonography

A new Presentation of the Principles of the Art - Part I, Fifth Edition

D. L. Scott-Browne

Scott-Browne's Text-Book of Phonography
A new Presentation of the Principles of the Art - Part I, Fifth Edition

ISBN/EAN: 9783337228514

Printed in Europe, USA, Canada, Australia, Japan

Cover: Foto ©ninafisch / pixelio.de

More available books at **www.hansebooks.com**

SCOTT-BROWNE'S
TEXT-BOOK of PHONOGRAPHY.

A NEW PRESENTATION OF THE PRINCIPLES OF
THE ART,

AS PRACTISED BY NINE-TENTHS OF THE MEMBERS OF THE PROFESSION IN AMERICA; AND THE ONLY WORK EMBODYING THE IMPROVEMENTS MADE IN THE LAST TEN YEARS.

FOR
SCHOOLS, COLLEGES AND PRIVATE INSTRUCTION.

BY
Mr. and Mrs. D. L. SCOTT-BROWNE,

TEACHERS OF THE ART FOR EIGHT YEARS IN THE COLLEGE OF PHONOGRAPHY; EDITORS OF "BROWNE'S PHONOGRAPHIC MONTHLY AND REPORTERS' JOURNAL" (ORGAN OF THE PROFESSION); AUTHORS OF THE AMERICAN STANDARD SERIES OF PHONOGRAPHIC TEXT-BOOKS; MEMBERS OF THE AMERICAN PHILOLOGICAL SOCIETY.

PART I.

FIFTH EDITION—REVISED.

NEW-YORK:
D. L. Scott-Browne,
1884.

PREFACE.

This work is a new, modern presentation of the principles of what is known as the STANDARD AMERICAN or BENN PITMAN SYSTEM OF FONOGRAFY (the most popular system in use), with, added thereto, such improvements as have, by the best fonografik scholars, teachers and practitioners of the art, been made and accepted during the past ten years, and which have never before been embodied in text-book form.

During the past five years this system, as herein presented, has been taught at SCOTT-BROWNE'S COLLEGE OF FONOGRAFY, New-York City, with the most gratifying results; and the gentlemen and ladies graduated at this institution, now occupying both professional and official positions, are among the most competent and successful shorthand writers in the country.

This work presents but one style of writing, equally suited to all uses required either by the amanuensis or verbatim reporter, and is, in every respect, the system best adapted to the acquirement and practise of the great mass of people for all business and reporting purposes, as its developement has been extended fartner, and contributed to by a greater number of minds, than any other, pre-eminently fitting it to be the standard system of shorthand writing in America.

The use of *f*, instead of *ph*, in the words fonografy, stenografy, etc., in this book, is in strict accordance with the orthografy of the Greek words from which they are derived; also, the dropping of final *e* in words where the preceding vowel is short, as in positiv, derivativ, etc., (sustaining one of our oldest orthographic rules), are both in agreement with the recommendation and *practise* of the Filological Societies of England and America.

THE AUTHORS.

Fonografik Headquarters,
   New-York City,
July, 1882.

CONTENTS.

Preface iii
To the Learner v
Definitions viii
CONSONANTS:—
    Lesson I.—Consonant Alfabet 1
VOWELS AND VOWELIZATION:—
    Lesson II.—Positiv and Relativ Values 6
    Lesson III.—Short Vowels 13
    Lesson IV.—Extra Vowels 17
    Punctuation, Capitals, Emphasis 18
    Lesson V.—Difthongs or Compound Vowels 19
    Lesson VI.—Joined Vowel Ticks 21
CIRCLES AND LOOPS:—
    Lesson VII.—Brief additional signs for *s* and *z* . . . 22
    Lesson VIII.—Loops for *st* and *str* 27
SEMICIRCLES AND HOOK:—
    Lesson IX.—Brief Signs for *Wa* and *Ya* 29
    Lesson X.—Brief *Wa* and *Ya* Signs disjoined . . . 32
ASPIRATE TICK, HEH:—
    Lesson XI.—Heh on stems 37
ABBREVIATIONS AND POSITION:—
    Lesson XII.—Abbreviations—Simple and Compound Stems . . 38
    Lesson XIII.—Abbreviations—Circles, Loops and Vowels . . 43
    Lesson XIV.—Abbreviations—Brief *Wa* and *Ya* Signs—Vowel, Stem, and Brief Sign Combination 46
HALF-LENGTHS AND ED TICK:—
    Lesson XV.—Halving Stems to add *t* or *d*—*ed* tick—Abbreviations . 48
INITIAL HOOKS:—
    Lesson XVI.—Small Initial Hooks for *l* and *r* on mated stems—*l* and *r* on unmated stems—Abbreviations 55
    Lesson XVII.—The Initial Circle on *l* and *r* hook signs—Abbreviations . 63
    Lesson XVIII—Back Hook for *in, en, un* 66
    Lesson XIX.—W-tick 67
    Lesson XX.—Small Terminal Hooks for *n f* and *v*—Abbreviations . 69
    Expression of Numbers 74
    Lesson XXI.—*Shun* and *Eshun* Hooks—Abbreviations . . 75
SHADING AND LENGTHENING:—
    Lesson XXII.—Shading *Em*—lengthening *ing*—lengthening other curves and *Ra* and *Hah*—Abbreviations 78
PREFIXES AND AFFIXES:—
    Lesson XXIII.—Prefixes—Compound Prefixes . . . 81
    Lesson XXIV.—Affixes—Abbreviations as Affixes . . . 85
ANALOGY AND PHRASING:—
    Lesson XXV.—Analogy—Phrasing 88

TO THE LEARNER.

IN taking up the study of Fonografy the learner must understand, from the start, that he is to lay aside the methods of both spelling and writing words as taught in our books and dictionaries; and that he must place himself in the attitude of a child who is just beginning to learn his A B C. There are two reasons for this advice:

1st.—The fonografik alfabet, unlike the one in our spelling books, contains as many letters or signs as there are elements or sounds in the English language, and not one of these letters or signs stands for more than one sound or value, hence, every word is to be spelled by just those letters or signs that represent the sound heard in the word—*one* sign for each sound, and no more. For example, the word *talk* is composed of *three* sounds, or elements, *t-aw-k;* *speak* is composed of four elements, *s-p-e-k;* *back*, three elements, *b-a-k;* *laugh*, three elements, *l-ah-f;* etc. So, in fonografy, there must be just as many signs used in spelling a word as there are elements, or sounds, heard in the pronunciation of the word; *three* signs in spelling *talk*, because there are but *three* elements heard; *four* signs in *speak*, because there are but *four* elements heard; and so on, in this way with all the words in the language.

2d.—The letters or signs of the fonografik alfabet are all *new* and unfamiliar to the learner, the same as *a b c* are new and unfamiliar to the child just learning them, and must be acquired in the same way—by memorizing. The child memorizes principally by the *repeating* process. The adult shortens this process by bringing his mind—his judgment—his reasoning powers—to his assistance. He calls to his aid all the ideas that he can associate in any way with the lessons he is learning, that could avail him any thing in acquiring them. The more intelligent the student, the more will he *learn by this law of association of ideas.*

The quickest way to learn the alfabet is, First: read it over, noticing the *name, sound, form, direction* and *thickness* or *shading* of each sign. Second: read carefully what is said about the *manner of writing* the stems—whether upward or downward, etc., following the directions given in the TEXT-BOOK, on page 2. Third: write the first eight stems of the alphabet, making and naming them in pairs, accenting the second one of each pair, and repeating words to rhyme with them as follows:

Pe *Be*, Te *De*, Cha *Ja*, Ka *Ga;*
This *is* for *me* to *learn* this *day*.

Also notice that the stems are arranged in the same regular order as the spokes of a wheel, and that there is a *thin* and *thick* or *light* and *heavy* spoke to each direction, thus: ⟋ ⟍ ⟍ which, paired thus: ⟍⟋ and separated without breaking their order, appear just as they are seen in the alfabet:

Pe *Be*, Te *De*, Cha *Ja*, Ka *Ga*.
This *is* for *me* to *learn* this *day*.

Then write the next eight stems, making and naming them also in pairs, and repeating words that will rhyme with them:

Ef *Ve*, Ith *The*, Es *Ze*, Ish *Zhe;*
This *too*, for *me* to *learn*, you *see*.

The remaining stems are unmated and divided into triplets, with words to rhyme, as follows:

La Er *Ra*, Em Un *Ing;*
Did you *say* I might *sing?*
Wa Ya Hah.
Yes, ha-*ha!*

Write the alfabet in SCOTT-BROWNE'S FONOGRAFIK COPY BOOK, following the directions therein given. The last alfabet exercise in the Copy-Book being like the one on page 3 of this book. If the Copy-Book is not used, any blank note-book will do, taking care to have the exercises neatly and correctly written.

At this point ask *why* some of the stems are mated—differing only in being *light* and *heavy*. Answer. Because the elements or sounds represented by the stems of each mated pair are formed alike in the mouth, and *are* alike, with the exception that the light ones, *p*, *t*, etc., are *whispered*, while their mates or cognates, *b*, *d*, etc., are *voiced*—the voice being heard before the lips separate to give them utterance. Therefore the *whispered* mated elements are represented by light lines—light *sound*, light *stem*—and the *voiced* mated elements by *heavy* lines—heavy *sound*, heavy *stem*. Pronouncing the syllables *ap*, *ab; at*, *ad; ach*, *aj; ak*, *ag;* etc., will enable the student to preceive, at once, **both** the similarity and difference between the mated elements.

The unmated elements are all voiced except *Hah*, and are represented by the curved stems that remained after the mated stems were provided for.

PENS AND PENCILS.

Practise with either pen or pencil. It is better to be familiar with the use of both. Let the pen be fine, and the ink clear and black. Hold the pen loosely so that it can be turned easily in writing the outlines of words containing stems made in different directions. Some reporters hold the pen or pencil between the first and second fingers. It is a good way, as the pen is more easily controlled and it enables one to write longer without fatigue. Both this and the usual way are recommended—each as a rest to the other. Of pencils graded by numbers, use No. 3; of Dixon's pencils, use those marked S. M. (Soft Medium); of the American Fonografic Pencils, use those marked S (Soft).

TIME REQUIRED TO LEARN PHONOGRAPHY.

Directions faithfully followed and lessons thoroughly learned, together with an hour's daily practise, will enable the average student to master this book in about two months. A month's additional practise, of from two to three hours daily, from another's reading—using any common school reading books (from Second to Fourth—omitting all the poetry), and good business letters—will fit the student to begin the work of receiving dictations of business letters, provided he can *spell, punctuate* and *write* longhand, or operate a writing machine well. These three are positiv pre-requisites in a shorthand amanuensis.

HOW AND WHEN TO PRACTISE.

In writing after another's reading let the same matter be repeated three times, at least. This enables the writer to criticise his first effort, make corrections, choose better forms for words, and improve generally the appearance of the second effort. The third effort confirms the corrections and improvements of the second and advances one's speed. After writing any thing the third time let the shorthand notes be *read* as many as two or three times and written out in longhand *once*. Repetition in writing and reading practise, is one of the secrets of gaining speed in writing and readiness in reading. As progress is made in correctness and speed of writing, the repeating practice can be gradually discontinued. Let the student *always* read every thing he writes. One's own notes, after becoming able to write easily, make better reading exercises than engraved fonografy. Amanuenses and reporters will have no trouble in reading their notes if, during the preparatory course, they faithfully read every thing they write.

DEFINITION OF FONOGRAFY, ETC.

FONOGRAFY (Phonography).—Any system of writing language in which only *the* SOUNDS *of the* SPOKEN *word are represented.*

STENOGRAFY.—Any system of shorthand writing, using brief alfabetic signs, arbitrary characters, principles of contraction, etc., adequate to the representation and speed of verbatim speech. The term is applied to systems of un-fonetik shorthand.

STENO-FONOGRAFY.—Any system of fonetic shorthand employing the alfabetik signs of stenography, principles of abbreviation and contraction, devices, etc., adequate to the representation and speed of verbatim speech.

FONETIKS (Phonetics).—The science of the sounds of the human voice.—(Webster.)

FONETIK (Phonetic) or Fonik (Phonic).—Relating to the representation of sounds by characters.—(Webster.)

Fonetik or *Fonik Shorthand* and *Steno-Fonografy* both mean one and the same thing.

The system of Shorthand or Stenografy taught in this book is fonetik or fonografik, and, hence, like all other systems having a fonetik basis, is termed, for brevity, *Fonografy* instead of *Steno-Fonografy*, there being no longhand fonografy to require the other as a distinguishing name.

PRONUNCIATION OF NATURE, QUESTION, ETC.

The theoretical pronunciation of the words *nature, future, question, fixture*, etc., is not so conveniently or quickly represented in fonografy as the popular pronunciation; therefore this work sanctions the fonografik writing of *nachur, fuchur, queschun, fixchur*, etc. If the reporter is to write what he *hears*, he will seldom have occasion to represent other than the popular pronunciation given to this class of words.

LESSON I.
1.—CONSONANT ALFABET.

	Fonografik Stem or Letter.	Name.	Sound.			Power.
		\multicolumn{4}{l	}{STRAIGHT STEMS (Mated).}	
ABRUPT ELEMENTS.	\	Pe	p	as in	....	.... u*p*
	|	Be	b	,,	....	.... a*b*
	|	Te	t	,,	....	.... i*t*
	|	De	d	,,	....	.... ai*d*
	/	Cha	ch	,,	....	.... ea*ch*
	/	Ja	j	,,	....	*j*oy, a*g*e, e*dg*e
	—	Ka	k	,,	....	oa*k*, *c*oo, e*ch*o
	—	Ga	g	,,	....	....e*gg*, e*g*o
		\multicolumn{4}{l	}{CURVED STEMS (Mated).}	
CONTINUANT ELEMENTS.	\\	Ef	f	as in	....	i*f*, lau*gh*, *ph*ase
	\\	Ve	v	,,	....	e*v*e, Ste*ph*en
	(	Ith	th	,	....	.... oa*th*
	(	The	dh	,,	....	.... *th*e
	)	Es	s	,,	....	.... u*s*, a*ce*
	)	Ze	z	,,	....	.... oo*ze*, a*s*
	∫	Ish	sh	,,	....	a*sh*, o*ce*an
	∫	Zhe	zh	,,	....	.... a*z*ure
		\multicolumn{4}{l	}{CURVED AND STRAIGHT STEMS (NOT MATED).}	
LIQUID ELEMENTS.	⌢ upward	La	l	as in	....	.... a*l*e
	⌢	Er	r	,,	....	.... ea*r*
	⁄ upward	Ra	r	,,	....	.... *r*oa*r*
NASAL ELEMENTS.	⌒	Em	m	,,	....	.... ai*m*
	⌣	Un	n	,,	....	.... a*n*
	⌣	Ing	ng	,,	....	.... so*ng*
COALESCENT ELEMENTS.	⌒	Wa	w	,,	....	.... *w*ay
	⌒	Ya	y	,,	....	.... *y*ou
ASPIRATE.	⁄ upward	Hah	h	,,	....	.... *h*ay

MANNER OF WRITING THE STEMS.

2. The Stems \ *Pe,* \ *Be,* | *Te,* | *De,* / *Cha,* / *Ja,* are written *downward.*

3. ⎯ *Ka,* ⎯ *Ga,* are written from *left* to *right.*

4. \ *Ef,* \ *Ve,* (*Ith,* (*The,*) *Es,*) *Ze,*) *Zhe,* are written *downward.*

5.) *Ish* is written downward when it is the only stem in a word, but when joined to other stems may be written either *upward* or *downward,* according to rules given in advanced lessons. When written upward it is named *Sha.*

6. (*La* is written upward when it is the only stem in a word, but when joined to other stems may be written either *upward* or *downward,* according to rules given in advanced lessons. When written downward it is named *El.*

7. \ *Er* is always written *downward.*

8. / *Ra* is always written *upward.*

9. ⌒ *Em,* ⌣ *Un,* ⌣ *Ing,* are written from *left* to *right.*

10. \ *Wa,* (*Ya,* are written *downward.*

11. / *Hah* is always written *upward.*

RESUMÉ.

a.) *Ish,* written *downward* when it is the only stem in a word. Written either *upward* or *downward,* according to certain rules, when joined to other stems. *Upward* name, *Sha.*

b. (*La,* written *upward* when it is the only stem in a word. Written either *upward* or *downward,* according to certain rules, when joined to other stems. *Downward* name, *El.*

c. / *Ra,* / *Hah,* always written *upward.*

d. ⎯ *Ka,* ⎯ *Ga,* ⌒ *Em,* ⌣ *Un,* ⌣ *Ing,* written from *left* to *right.*

e. All the other stems invariably written *downward.*

NOTE.—Trace and name every one of the stems on page 1 several times; after which, practise writing them in "Scott-Browne's Phonographic Copy-Book," page 1.

12.—EXERCISE TO BE WRITTEN IN COPY-BOOK.

Pe,	Be,	
Te,	De,	
Cha,	Ja,	
Ka,	Ga,	
Ef,	Ve,	
Ith,	The,	
Es,	Ze,	
Ish,	Zhe,	
La *or* El,		
Er,		
Ra,		
Em,		
Un,		
Ing,		
Wa,		
Ya,		
Hah.		

NOTE.—For practise on this exercise see page 2 of "Phonographic Copy-Book."

MANNER OF JOINING CONSONANT STEMS.

13. When two or more stems are used in the outline of a word, they are written without lifting the pen; the next beginning where the preceding one ends. Illustration:

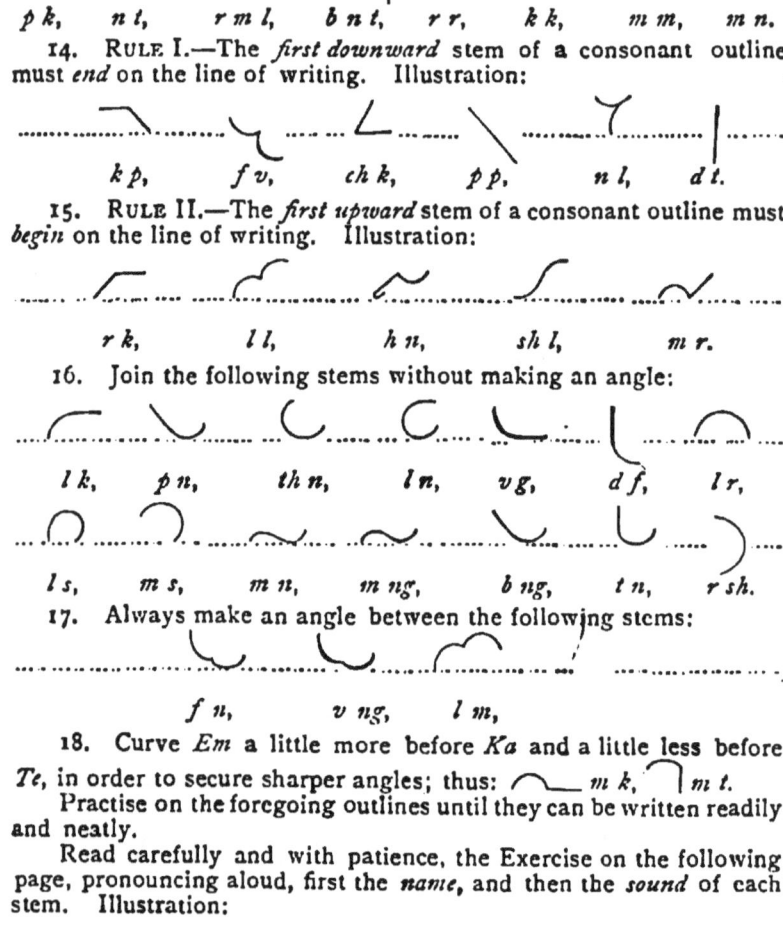

p k, n t, r m l, b n t, r r, k k, m m, m n.

14. RULE I.—The *first downward* stem of a consonant outline must *end* on the line of writing. Illustration:

k p, f v, ch k, p p, n l, d t.

15. RULE II.—The *first upward* stem of a consonant outline must *begin* on the line of writing. Illustration:

r k, l l, h n, sh l, m r.

16. Join the following stems without making an angle:

l k, p n, th n, l n, v g, d f, l r,

l s, m s, m n, m ng, b ng, t n, r sh.

17. Always make an angle between the following stems:

f n, v ng, l m,

18. Curve *Em* a little more before *Ka* and a little less before *Te*, in order to secure sharper angles; thus: *m k, m t.*

Practise on the foregoing outlines until they can be written readily and neatly.

Read carefully and with patience, the Exercise on the following page, pronouncing aloud, first the *name*, and then the *sound* of each stem. Illustration:

NAMES.   SOUNDS.

Pe-Em   *p m,* sounding the *p* as in *ape*, leaving off the *e; m* as in *me*, leaving off *e*.

NOTE.—For practise on this exercise see page 3 of "Phonographic Copy-Book."

19.—READING EXERCISE.

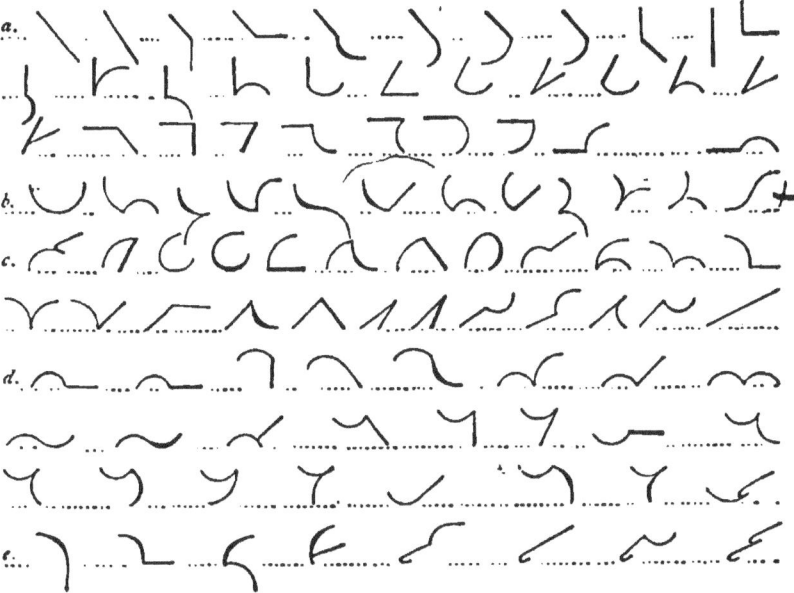

20. The hook on *Hah* cannot be made perfectly when *Hah* is joined to *Ja*, *Ya*, etc., but an imperfect hook or *offset* is made on the stems, which is just as legible to the student as the complete hook, after becoming familiar with it.

The above Reading Exercise contains the correct consonant outlines of the following words:

21.—WRITING EXERCISE.

a. Pope, pub, pity, pick; bevy, busy, bush, bijou; Tabby, tidy, tag; daisy, duly, door, dame, deny; check, China, cherry; Johnny, gem, jury, Jehu; keep, Cady, cage, coffee; Goth, Gussie, gush, gaily

b. Fish, fame; vale, valley, veer, vary; theme, thorough; sewer; zeal; sham, shallow.

c. Lehigh, lodge, Lena, lung, league, love, lobby, Lizzie, Laura, Alma; arm, ark, early, Aurora; rock, review, rib, rich, ridge, rash, rely, wreath, renew, rear.

d. Make, mug, meadow, map, move, mail, Mary, maim, money, among, Mayhew; nap, into, inch, nag, enough, knoweth, noisy, Nash, nail, narrow, anyway, N. Y. (*En-Ya*), N. H. (*En-Hah*).

e. Await, awoke, Oyer, Yahoo; holy, Harry, honey, ha-ha.

NOTE.—Practise on pages 4 and 5 of "Scott-Browne's Phonographic Copy-Book."

VOWELS AND VOWELIZATION.

LESSON II.
POSITIV AND RELATIV VALUES.

1. The *sound* for which any sign or letter stands is called the *value* or *power* of that sign or letter; and if that sign or letter never stands for any other value or power—never changes its value, but always keeps the same—that value is termed *fixed*, or *positiv*, or *absolute*,—all three of these words being in use to express the same idea. It has been observed in the foregoing lesson that the values of the fonografik (phonographic) consonant-signs are positiv, fixed, unchanging; that is, p is always *p*, and d always *d*, wherever they are written, and never stand for the sound of *f* or *t* or any other value than each its own.

2. But in this lesson it will be noticed that the values of the *simple* vowel signs are not positiv, but are dependent upon their *relation to the consonant stem* for their values. To illustrate: A heavy dot written opposit the *beginning* of a stem thus, ❘ , is called *e*, but if this same dot is moved down opposit the *middle* of the stem, thus, •❘ , it is called *a*, and if moved again down opposit the *end* of the stem, thus, ₊❘ , it is called *ah;* thus forming a short scale of three sounds, *e, a, ah*,—the consonant stem being of a convenient size to furnish three distinctly different vowel sounds. By this, then, it is seen that the *simple* vowel signs do not have *fixed* values, as it can not be known what to call a dot till it has been *placed* by the side of a stem; hence, it is said that the vowel signs possess *relativ* value; that is, their *relation* to the stem must be shown before it can be known what sound, or value, to giv them.

3. The vowel signs, then, possess *not positiv* but *relativ* value, and are represented by *dots* and *dashes* written in three different places by the side of the consonant stem, and made *heavy* and *light* to correspond with *long* and *short* vowel sounds. *Heavy* signs for *long* vowels and *light* signs for *short* ones.

THE VOWEL SCALE, OR ALFABET.

4. There are, in the English language, sixteen *simple* vowel elements—six long, and ten short,—and seven *compound* vowels, or difthongs, as heard in the following words:—

LONG VOWELS.

B*e*, *e*rr, f*a*re, f*a*r, f*a*ll, m*o*ve.

SHORT VOWELS.

*I*t, *e*ll, *u*p, c*u*r, *a*t, *a*sk, l*o*g, wh*o*le, w*o*lf, and i̯,*
the initial element of the difthong, i̯-ŏŏ, heard in the words *blue, rue, rude, tune, suit,* etc.

COMPOUND VOWELS, OR DIFTHONGS.

*A*le, *o*ld, *i*ce, *oi*l, *ow*l, tr*u*e, p*u*re.

5. For practical reporting purposes it is not found necessary to represent each of these elements with a distinct sign of its own. Eighteen signs are regarded sufficient—fourteen *simple* and four *compound* signs. Two of the seven difthongs—*a* and *o*—are, for reasons not necessary to explain here, classed, in fonografy (phonography), with the simple vowels and represented by simple signs.

LONG VOWELS AND THEIR SIGNS.

6. The six long vowels (including *a* and *o*), classed together, are as follows:

| e | a | ah | aw | o | oo |

and represented thus:

•｜	•｜	•｜	─｜	─｜	─｜
e	a	ah	aw	o	oo
W*e*	g*a*ve	*a*lms	*a*ll	c*o*ld	f*oo*d.

7. When a vowel sign is written opposit the *beginning* of a stem it is said to be in the *first place;* when opposit the *middle* of a stem, in the *second place;* when opposit the *end* of a stem, the *third place.*

8. Observe that the *beginning* or *first place*, of a vowel, is where the stem *begins to be written.* The *first place* of *Pe, Cha, Ef, Ith,* etc., is at the *top* because that is where those stems *begin;* while the *first place* of *La, Ra, Hah,* is at the *bottom,* because that is where those stems begin. (See next page, lines 2-7, first and fourth columns.)

9. The dash signs are written at right angles to the consonant stem; that is, in an *opposit direction* to that of the stem. (See next page, fourth, fifth and sixth columns.)

10. The consonant portion of a word is written first and the vowel portion afterwards.

---

* This sound is *formed* in the mouth like the vowel in *it*, but *uttered* like the vowel in *up*, from the *back* of the mouth, with the throat as nearly in position for sounding ŭ (in *up*) as the tongue can allow and preserve the *form* of ĭ (in *it*).

11.—EXERCISE ON LONG VOWELS.

	DOTS.			DASHES.		
	BEGINNING.	MIDDLE.	END.	BEGINNING.	MIDDLE.	END.
1.	1st place.	2nd place.	3rd place.	1st place.	2nd place.	3rd place.
	W-*e*	g-*a*-ve	*ah* / *a*-lms	*aw* / *a*-ll	*o* / c-*o*-ld	*oo* / f-*oo*-d
2.	Te	ta	tab	taw	toe	too
3.	Key	kay	kah	caw	coe	coo
4.						
5.						
6.						
7.						
8.	Eat	ate	aht	awt	oat	oot
9.	Eke	ache	ahk	awk	oak	ook
10.						
11.						
12.						

12. RULE III.—Vowels that are read *before* a consonant are written to the *left* of vertical and inclined stems, the same as they would be in longhand, and *above* horizontal stems, the same as an *upper line of writing* reads before a *lower line*. Illustration:

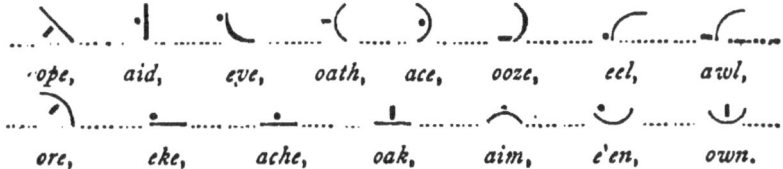

ope, aid, eve, oath, ace, ooze, eel, awl,

ore, eke, ache, oak, aim, e'en, own.

13. RULE IV.—Vowels that are read *after* a consonant are written to the *right* of vertical and inclined stems, and *below* horizontal stems. Illustration:

bow, tea, dough, fee, sow, shoe, law, ray, hah,

key, coo, gay, may, ma, knee, neigh, gnaw, know.

14. In naming the letters, or signs, of fonografik (phonographic) words, be careful to get the exact sound for each sign, and, after spelling the words by their correct sounds, be doubly careful to pronounce them exactly as they were spelled. Illustration:

    a-p, *ape*, and not *ăp;*
    t-a-m, *tame*, and not *tăm;*
    d-o-m, *dome*, and not *dŏm;*
    t-a-k, *take*, not *tack;*
    b-a-k, *bake*, not *back;*
    r-a-t, *rate*, not *rat.*

In this way, carefully spell, both by sound and name of each sign, and pronounce, correctly, the fonografik words on page 11.

15. Do not allow the common, printed spelling to mislead when spelling a word in fonografy. Illustration:

Ache, *ā-k*, and not *a-se-aitch-e;*

coo, *k-ōō*, and not *se-double-o;*

thaw, *Ith-aw,* not *te-aitch-a-doubleyou;*

eel, *e-l,* not *double-e-l;*

talk, *t-aw-k,* not *t-a-el-k;*

though, *The-o,* not *t-aitch-o-you-je-aitch;*

gale, *Ga-a-l,* not *je-a-l-e;*

shawl, *Ish-aw-l,* not *Es-aitch-a-doubleyou-l;*

rouge, *Ra-ōō-Zhe,* not *ar-o-you-je-e.*

cage, *k-a-j,* not *se-a-je e.*

16. Write no more signs in a word than there are sounds heard in its pronunciation. Silent letters seen in printed words are never represented in fonografy. Illustration: Know, *n-o* ‒ ⌄; gnaw, *n-aw* ‒ ⌒; see, *s-e* ‒); cope, *k-o-p* ‒ ⌐\

17. Before writing a word in fonografy pronounce it slowly and then sound all the elements *separately,* heard in the slow pronunciation, in order to determine the *exact sounds,* and the *correct signs* to be written. Illustration:

Word.	Slow pronunciation.	Separate sounds.	Names of consonant stems.	Stem outline.	Name of each sound.	Full word
Zero,	z e r o,	z-e-r-o,	Ze-Ra	⌐	Ze-e-Ra-o	⌐
Dado,	d a d o,	d-a-d-o,	De-De	|	De-a-De-o	|⁻
Cocoa,	c o c oa,	k-o-k-o,	Ka-Ka	‒‒‒	Ka-o-Ka-o	‒‒‒
Delay,	d e l ay,	d-e-l-a,	De-La	⌐	De-e-La-a	⌐

NOTE.—Remember that the pen must not be lifted till all the consonant stems of an outline are written, after which the vowel signs are placed.

18.—READING EXERCISE
ON LONG VOWELS.

1st Place Vowels.

2nd Place Vowels.

3rd Place Vowels.

19.—WRITING EXERCISE

ON THE LONG VOWELS.

Pea, pa, paw, Po, poo, ape, ope, bay, baa, bow, obey, eat, ate, oat, tea. aid, ode, day, dough, age, Jo, eke, ache, oak, key, coo, gay, fee, fay, foe, eve. oath, thaw, sou, ace, ooze, Shah, shaw, show, shoe, lee, lay, lo, eel, ale, awl, aim, ma, knee, gnaw, woe, woo. yah, yo, haw, hoe, hah.

Peep, pope, peach, poach, peak, poke, opaque, Peko, peal, pail, pale, Paul, pole, babe, beat, beet, bait, boat, beach, beak, bake, bail, ball, bowl, below, beam, tape, teach, teeth, tail, tall, toll, team, tame, deep, daub, dado, dale, dole, delay, deem, dame, dome, cheap, cheat, Choate, cheek, chalk, choke, Job, joke, jail, keep, cape, cope, coach, cage, cake, coke, keel, coal, comb, gale, goal, game, feed, fade, Feejee, faith, fame, foam, veto, evoke, vague, vogue, thief, thieve, theme, sheep, shape, Sheik, shake, zeal, leap, lobe, load, leach, liege, leak, lake, leaf, loaf, leave, loathe, leal, lame, leeway, mope, meek, mock, meal, male, mail, mole, maim, knave, 'neath, name, heap, heat, hate, heed, hoed, heath, halo, ho-ho, ha-ha.

Write *Ra* for *r* in the following words, because it is followed by a vowel:

Ray, raw, row, reap. rope, robe, rate, wrought, wrote, reed, raid, road, rowed, reach, rage, wreak, rake, rogue, wreath, wreathe, relay ream, roam, Rome, rear, roar, Reno, zero, Nero, hero.

Write *Er* for *r* in the following words, because it is preceded by a vowel:

Ore, oar, pier, peer, pour, bier, bore, tear, tore, deer, door, chore, jeer, fear, four, veer, shear, shore, leer, lore.

Write *El* (downward) for *l* in the following words, because it is final and preceded by either *f*, *v* or the upward *r*, in which case it must be written downward:

Fail, foal, veal, vale, reel, rail.

Write *Sha* and *La* (both upward) for *sh* and *l* in the following words, because they make the best joining:

Shawl, shoal, shield, leash.

LESSON III.

SHORT VOWELS.

1. The six short vowels, classed together, are heard in the following syllables:

  ĭ(t) ĕ(t) ă(t) ŏ(t) ŭ(t) ŏŏ(t)

and are represented thus:

ĭ	ĕ	ă	ŏ	ŭ	ŏŏ
Ĭt	fĕll	flăt ask	ŏn	pŭp's cŭr	foot

2. The six *long* and six *short* vowels may be easily memorized by repeating the following words containing them:

  W*e* gave *a*lms—*a*ll c*o*ld f*oo*d.
   ē ā ą ā ō ōō
   Ĭt fĕll ·flăt — ŏn pŭp's fŏŏt.
   ĭt ĕt ăt ŏt ŭt ŏŏt

3. Rules for writing vowels heard *between* STEM CONSONANTS:

RULE V.—ALL *first place* and the two long *second place* vowels, *a* and *o*, are written *after* the *first* consonant. Illustration:

  peak *big* *talk* *dock* *bake* *dome* *cake* *comb.*

RULE VI.—ALL the *third place* and the two SHORT *second place* vowels, *ĕ* and *ŭ*, are written *before* the *second* consonant. Illustration:

  palm *boom* *tack* *took* *neck* *numb*

NOTE.—If *first place* vowels were written *before* the *second* stem, and *third place* vowels *after* the *first* stem, it would bring the vowel signs within the angles, and then it could not be told whether the vowel was a *first* place one to the *second* stem or a *third* place one to the *first* stem. Illustration:  It cannot be told whether the first word is *balm* or *beam*, or the second word, *pack* or *pick*; but by applying Rule V. the following word, ⌒ , is known to be *beam,* and by applying Rule VI. this word, ⌒ , is known to be *balm.*

4. The second place vowels could be written to either stem, but to make an equal division of the signs to each stem it was thought best by Mr. Pitman to write the long ones to the *first* and the short ones to the *second* stem, which added to the legibility of such words as ⌒ *bake,* ⌒ *beck,* ⌐ *dome,* ⌐ *dumb,* etc., when in careless or rapid writing the size of the vowel was not accurate.

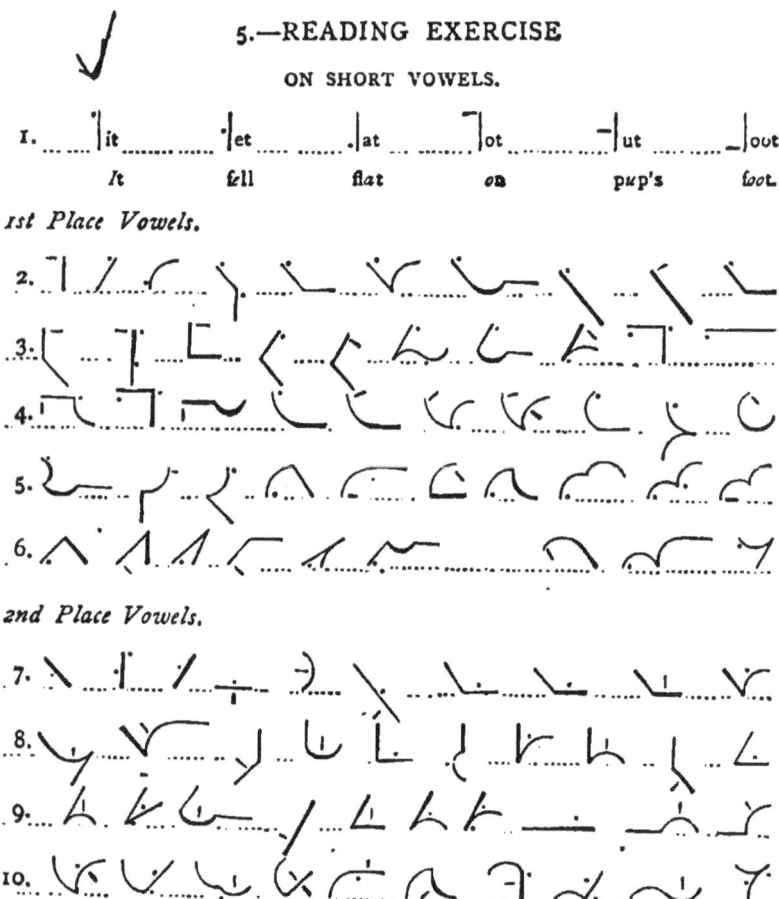

5.—READING EXERCISE

ON SHORT VOWELS.

1. it et at ot ut out
   It fell flat on pup's foot.

1st Place Vowels.

2.

3.

4.

5.

6.

2nd Place Vowels.

7.

8.

9.

10.

3rd Place Vowels.

11.
12.
13.
14.

6.—WRITING EXERCISE
ON SHORT VOWELS.

Ebb, abby, odd, eddy, add, itch, etch, edge, echo, egg, ash, ill, ell, Ella, alley, Emma, Anna, pity, petty, patty, putty, pod, pitch, patch, pick, peck, pack, Puck, pig, pygmy, peg, pug, pith, pussy, push, pill, pull, pully, pink, batch, badge, budge, back, book, big, beg, bag, bog, bug, buggy, bevy, busy, bush, bushy, bijou, bill, billow, bell, ballêt (ballay), bung, tip, tap, top, tub, attach, touch, tick, tack, attack, tuck, attic, tag, tug, taffy, tally, tarry, Tenney, tung, tank, dip, ditty, oddity, dig, dog, dug, death, doth, dell, dull, dally, doll, dim, dumb, ding, dong, chip, chap, chop, chat, chick, check, chill, chilly, chimney, chink, jib, job, jet, jut, Judd, judge, Jack, jockey, jig, jag, jog, jug, gill, jelly, jolly, gem, Jennie, Johnnie, Kipp, cab, cob, cub, Kitty, catch, cudgel, Cudjo, kick, cook, keg, cog, coffee, café, kith, cash, calla, callow, king, kink, gig, gag, Goth, gush, galley, gull, gully, gum, guinea, gang, gong, fob, fitch, fetch, fudge, fag, fog, foggy, fellow, fallow, follow, Fanny, funny, fang, valley, volley, vim, thatch, thick, thicket, thumb, thong, zinc, ship, shop, shabby, shadow, shock, shook, shaggy, sham, shank, lip, lap, lop, elbow, Libby, lobby, lad, laddie, ledge, allege, lodge, lick, lack, lock, locket, luck, lucky, look, live, love, lofty, loth, lilly, loll, lull, limb, lamb, rally, map, mop, mob, Mattie, meadow, match, mock, muck, mug, miff, muff, myth, moth, mash, mush, mashed, mill, milk, mellow, mum, mummy, Minnie, Moony, many, monk, nip, nap, knap, nib, knob, Netie, niche, notch, nudge, nick, neck, knack, knock, nook, knag, nag, gnash, unlucky, ninny, Nancy,

Write *Ra* for *r* in the following words, because *Ra* is to be used when the directions for *Ar* do not apply: Perry, parry, bury, berry, cherry, ferry, rip, rap, rot, rut, rid, red, rich, wretch, rack, rook, rig, rug, ring, merry, marry, enrich, Harry, hurry, rim, rum.

Write *Er* for *r* in the following words: Erie, aerie, Ehrich.

Write *El* (downward) for *l* in the following words: Kingly, rill, knell, null, annul, ilk elk, alack, leg, lag, log, lug, Ilm, elm, Elmo, alum, Alma, Olney, Lena, Ilion, lung, link, lank.

Write *Sha*, *La* and *Ra* (all upward) for *sh*, *l* and *r* in the following words: Shell, shallow, lash, lashed, polish, polished abolish abolished, rash, rush, hash, hush.

The following directions add to the legibility of Phonography.

Ar is used when preceded by a vowel, thus: and when it is final, thus: except when it is immediately followed by / or / and then

Ra / must be used, thus: and always use *Ra* when the sound of *r* follows or (thus: and for an additional *r* sound preceded by the *Ka* sign, thus: and where *r* follows Hah thus: See the engravings of *Ar* and *Ra* thruout the book.

El (downward *l*) must always be used when preceded by a vowel and followed by ___ ___ or thus: ; when final immediately following or thus: ; when preceded by or thus: ; and when followed by the consonants ___ or thus: because the joining is most easily made.

La (upward *l*) is used in all other cases and also where derivativ words are required to be written in analogy with their primitivs thus: and where modifying principles would require the upward *l* for legibility of outline, which will be seen in the engravings of more advanced lessons.

LESSON IV.

EXTRA VOWELS
AND THEIR SIGNS.

1. The vowels *ē* in *her* and *â* in *dare* are not classed in their proper places with the other long vowels, partly on account of such an arrangement breaking up the usual six-vowel order of long and short vowels, and partly because some fonografik authors do not provide for their representation, but use as substitutes either the second place *light* dot *ĕ* for the sound of *e* in *her* and *i* in *sir* or the *light* dash *ŭ* for *u* in *cur*, and the second place *heavy* dot *a* for the vowel in *dare*. It is much better that these distinct sounds have distinct signs of their own, and this book provides proper representation for them as follows:

2. A light dash written in *second place*, parallel with the stem for the vowel in *her, sir*, etc., and in *third place*, parallel with the stem, for the vowel in *dare*. Illustration: *err* *Goethe* (Ge(r)tuh), *air,* *fairy.*

3. The vowel in *ask, past, alas*, etc., is the true short mate of the vowel in *far*, the correct sign for which is the *third place light dot* used also to represent the sharper vowel heard in *rat*, which is the short mate of the vowel heard in *air, dare*, etc. On account of the similarity of these two vowels it is not necessary, for reporting purposes, to have two distinct signs. Should a distinct sign be required, in order to teach exact pronunciation, the *light* third place parallel dash can be used to represent the short vowel in *rat*, and the same sign made heavy to represent the long vowel in *dare*.

4. The vowel heard in *cur, work, journey*, etc., is more of a guttural than the one heard in *earnest, mercy, girl*, etc., and is represented by the second place light dash, as in *cup*.

5.—READING EXERCISE
ON EXTRA VOWELS.

6.—WRITING EXERCISE.

ON EXTRA VOWELS.

Goethe, Percy, (*Ra* for *r*), mercy.

Write *Er* for *r* in the following words:

Herb, herbage, herbal, earl, early, ergo, air, airy, pair, pare, pear, bear, bare, barely, tare, dare, Adair, fare, fair, affair, lair.

Write *Ra* for *r* in the following words: Fairy, Thayer, rare, mare, rarer (three lengths of *Ra*), thus:

Fair day. Percy came early. Poor, cheap fare. Rare, early pear.

PUNCTUATION, CAPITALS, EMPHASIS.

1.—The punctuation marks used in fonografic writing are:

× or / .. PERIOD—Used at the end of complete sentences.

┴ ...... DASH—Used in a break of sentences.

( ) .. PARENTHESIS—Used to enclose parenthetical remarks.

[ ] BRACKET—Used to enclose remarks by reporter or editor.

⌀ ...... HYPHEN—Used to indicate compound words.

..... EMPHASIS—Used to indicate emphatic words and sentences. .

.... CAPITALIZER—Used to denote capitalization or name, and the words *equal to*.

.... PLEASANTRY OR LAUGHTER—Used to denote mirthful feeling.

× .... INTERROGATION—Used to denote a question.

× .... EXCLAMATION—Used to indicate feeling, pathos, wonder or surprise.

All other punctuation marks used in writing and printing must be supplied in the transcripts made of one's shorthand notes.

2.—Capital letters are indicated thus:

E, O, N. Y., Lima.

3.—In letter writing, or in memoranda, the vowel initials of names, if preferred, can be expressed by their signs written in the correct vowel place by side of the cancelled *Te* stem, thus:

E, O.

4.—To indicate emphasis in print, words are set in italic letters. To indicate emphasis in longhand writing, words are underscored by a straight, horizontal line. To indicate emphasis in fonografic writing, words are underscored by a waved line. Illustration:

Best *merry*

LESSON V.

DIFTHONGS, OR COMPOUND VOWELS.

1.   　　ī　　　oi　　　ow　　　ew
　　　My　　boy's　　owl　　flew.

DIFTHONG SIGNS.

　　　＇　　　＞　　　＾　　　＜
　　　i　　　oi　　　ow　　　ew

2. The difthong signs are derived from the letter ✕, or inclined cross, thus:

$$\text{oi} \diagup\!\!\!\!\diagdown \text{ew}$$
　　　　ow

Observe that in writing these signs, the angle should be made sharper than is shown in the cross.

3. The difthong signs possess fixed values, and are written in the most convenient place,—usually the *third* place.

4. The difthong following *r*, as in *rude, rumor, rule*, etc., is not so sharp as that heard in *pure, cure, beauty*, etc., but the same sign is used to represent both.

5. Initial difthongs should be written first, and, if convenient, joined to the following stem. Illustration: *Ida*, *ivy*, *ice*.

6.—READING EXERCISE
ON DIFTHONGS.

20 SCOTT-BROWNE'S TEXT-BOOK

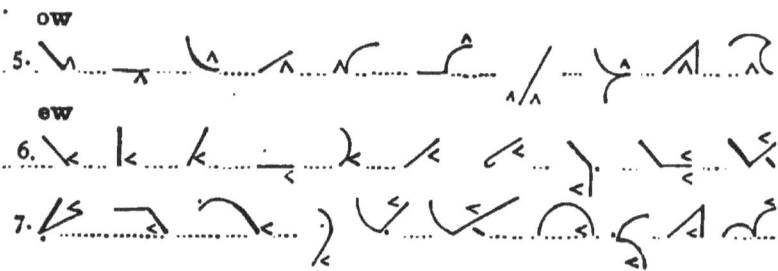

7.—WRITING EXERCISE
ON DIFTHONGS.

Pie, tie, Ida, Ike, Guy, fie, vie, ivy, thigh, sigh, ice, eyes, shy, lie, lye, ally, nigh, high, isle, aisle, pipe, pike, pile, abide, byway, tidy, tithe, time, tiny, dike, dime, idol, chime, China, jibe, kite, chyle, chyme, guide, guile, Fido, five, shiny, like, life, alive, lime, imbibe, mighty, mile, knife, hypo, height, hide.

Boy, boil, toy, toil, joy, coy, coil, Voy, avoid, alloy, oil, annoy, noisy, ahoy.

Bow, Dow, cow, vow, row, owl, owlish (*ow-La-Sha*), chow-chow, couch, gouge, fowl, foul, avowed, vouch, loud, mouth.

Pew, dew, adieu, due, chew, Jew, cue, thew, Sue, lieu, hew, hue, Hugh, huge, beauty, duty, dupe, duke, eschew, juror, juicy, July, Jehu, cube, imbue, mule.

Write *Er* for *r* in the following words: Ire, pyre, attire, dire, gyre (*Ja-Er*), fire, lyre, tire, Irish (*i-Er-Ish*), toiler, lure, allure (*El-Er*).

Write *Ka* for *r* in the following words: Rye, wry, ripe, right, rite, write, Wright, arrive, writhe, irate, aright, mire, roy, roil (*Ra-El*), roilly (*Ka-La*), rout, rowdy, rue, pursue, bureau, jury, fury, furore, rude, review.

Write *El* for *l* in the following words: File, Nile, foil, roil, Hoyle, fowl, foul.

LESSON VI.

JOINED VOWEL-TICKS.

1. A vowel (belonging either to the *dot* or *dash* class), following a difthong, is more quickly and conveniently represented by a small tick joined to the difthong sign, and written in the direction of *Te* on *oi* and *ew*, and of *Ka* on *i* and *ow*.

2.—READING EXERCISE
ON JOINED VOWEL TICKS.

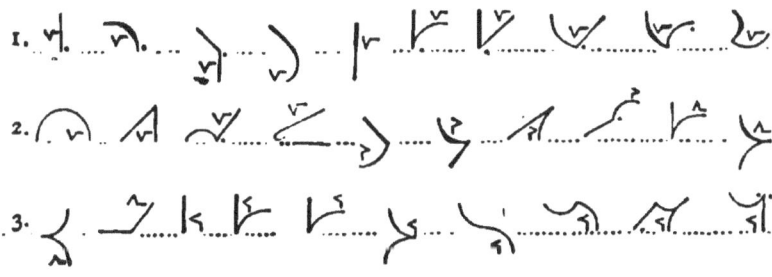

3.—WRITING EXERCISE
ON JOINED VOWEL TICKS.

Iota, Iowa, Iona, piety, pious, bias, Tioga, diet, dial, Viola, scion, Zion, boyish, coyish, voyage, towel, dewy, Dewey, Jewess, duel, dual, jewel, jewish, Shuey, annuity.

Write *Er* for *r* in the following words: Dyer, power, tower, dower, shower, jeweler, fewer, sewer, newer.

Write *Ra* for *r* in the following words: Diary, fiery, riot, Ryan, miry, higher, royal (*Ra-El*) royally (*Ra-La*), cower, Rowell (*Ra-El*), jewelry, ruin, renewal (*El* stem), hewer.

Write *El* for *l* in the following words: Vial, viol, lion, royal, vowel, Rowell, Howell, fuel, Newell, renewal.

CIRCLES AND LOOPS.

LESSON VII.

BRIEF ADDITIONAL SIGNS FOR S AND Z.

1. The frequently occurring sounds of *s* and *z* are, in a large class of words, represented by a small circle, o, named *Ĭs* or *Ĭz*, used at the beginning of stems, between stems, and at the end of stems, thus securing convenience in joining, brevity of outline, and greater ease and rapidity in writing.

2. The circle is joined to straight stems by a *leftward* motion of the pen, moving in three distinct directions, as shown in this little square joined initially to the *Pe* stem, ⟨ , while a fourth direction forms the stem.

3. The circle is always written on the concave side of a curve thus:

4. In joining the circle to *any* stem, either initially or finally, let the *first* and *last* movements be at *right angles* with the stem. Illustration:

Let the learner practise on the squares until without their aid a perfect circle can be easily formed.

5. The circle has no effect upon vowelization. A vowel heard either *before* or *after* a consonant represented by a *stem* is always written *before* or *after* the stem, whether a circle is on the stem or not. Illustration: *up*, *sup*, *pie*, *spy*, *eat*, *seat*, *ache*, *sake*.

6. A vowel is *never* read *before* an initial circle. The initial circle *always* reads *first*, and then any vowel that may be *before* the stem, and then the *stem*, and then any vowel that may *follow* the stem. Illustration: *settee*, *satiety*, *soda*. See page 24, line 4.

OF PHONOGRAPHY. 23

7. Initial *s* is expressed on the *Hah* stem by a circle in the place of the hook. Illustration: ⤴ *Soho*. See line 4, seventh and eighth words of page 24.

8. Initial *z* is always represented by the stem. See page 25, line 16.

9. The circle at the end of stems is always read last. A vowel cannot read *after* a circle because the circle furnishes no *places* in which three different vowels could be written. See page 24, line 5.

10. A circle between two straight stems running in the *same* direction, is written by the same motion of the pen as the circle on a single straight stem. See page 24, line 6.

11. A circle between straight stems, struck in different directions, is written *outside* of the angle. See page 24, line 7.

12. A circle between a straight line and a curve, is always written on the concave side of the curve. See page 25, line 8.

13. A circle between *Em* and any other curve, when it cannot come within the curve of *both* stems, is written on the concave side of *Em*. See page 25, line 9.

14. A circle between *Ef*, *Un*, and *La*, and between *La* and *Ve*, and *La* and *Ith*, is written on the concave side of *La*. See page 25, line 10.

15. The circle between other curve combinations is written on the concave side of both curves. See page 25, line 11.

LARGE CIRCLE FOR SES, SEZ, ZEZ.

16. The double sound of *s* or *z*—*ses*, *sez*, *zez*—is expressed by a *large* circle in such words as—

passes,   *possess*,   *teases*,   *possessed*,   *excessive*,   *races*.

17. The use of a double-sized circle to express the double sound of *s* and *z*, allows the plural ending of words to be formed in analogy with words in the singular number terminating with the small circle. Illustration:

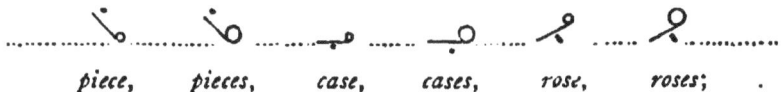

piece,   *pieces*,   *case*,   *cases*,   *rose*,   *roses*;   .

also the third person singular of such verbs as end with the small circle is expressed with the large circle. Illustration:

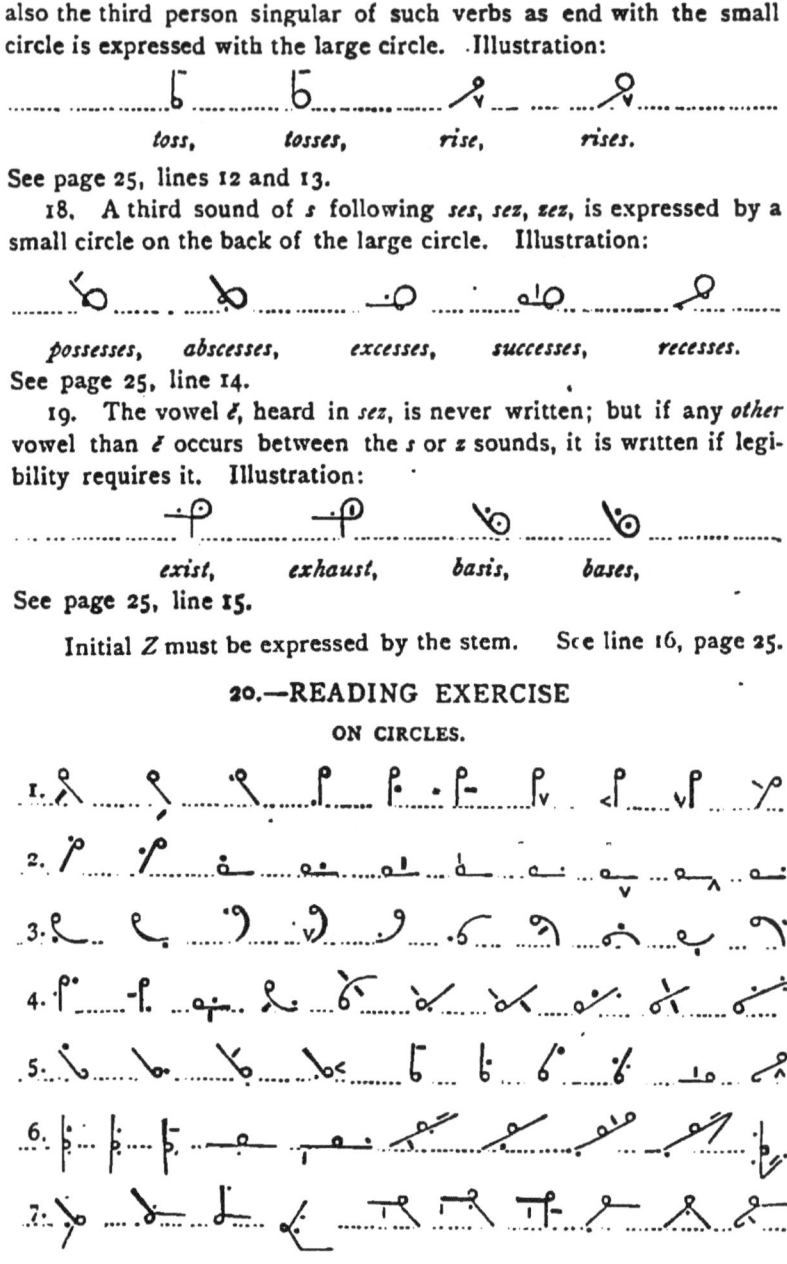

toss,   tosses,   rise,   rises.

See page 25, lines 12 and 13.

18. A third sound of *s* following *ses, sez, zez*, is expressed by a small circle on the back of the large circle. Illustration:

possesses,   abscesses,   excesses,   successes,   recesses.

See page 25, line 14.

19. The vowel *é*, heard in *sez*, is never written; but if any *other* vowel than *é* occurs between the *s* or *z* sounds, it is written if legibility requires it. Illustration:

exist,   exhaust,   basis,   bases,

See page 25, line 15.

Initial *Z* must be expressed by the stem. See line 16, page 25.

20.—READING EXERCISE
ON CIRCLES.

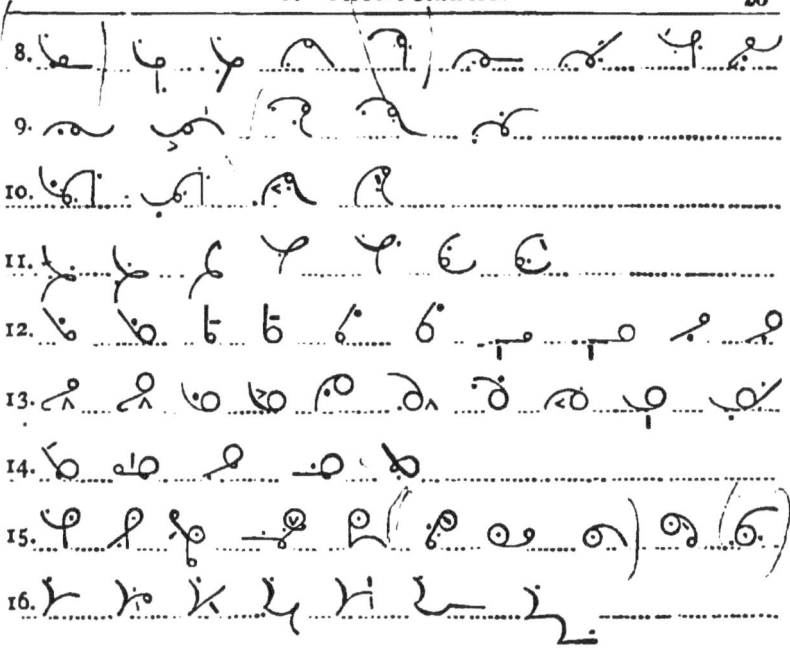

21.—WRITING EXERCISE
ON CIRCLES.

Soap, soup, sips, saps, seat, stays, stows, stew, suit, sight, sty, seed, said, sad, sawed, sowed, soda, suds, seeds, sage, sages, seige, sedge, sausages, seek, sake, sick, sacks, success, successes, Sussex, sag, sago, safe, sofa, save, seive, sythe, size, sizes, seize, seizes, sash, sashes, seal, seals, sails, sale, solo, sorry, sorrows, sore, sere, sour, sire, sir, Sam, seam, sum, psalm, sin, son, sun, sane, sign, sneeze, snows, sing, sang, sung, sway, sways, Swiss, Soho, Sahara.

Pass, piece, peace, passes, pieces, pace, paces, pause, pauses, posses, possesses, base, bays, boys, abase, abases, abuse, abscess, abscesses, tease, teases, days, dose, doze, dozes, disease, diseases, cheese, cheeses, chase, chews, etches, ages, joys, Jews, juice, rejoice, rejoices, kiss, kisses, Cass, Cass's, case, cases, oaks, aches, echoes, ox, ax, axes, axis, axes, excess, excesses, excuse, excuses, exercise, exercises, exercised, guess, guesses, gaze, geese, goose, gas, gases, gauze, Guy's, face, faces, vase, vases, vice, vices, voice, voices vows, views, reviews, thighs, oaths, shows, shoes, ashes, lace, laces, loose, looses, lose, loses, lease, allays, alleys, Ellis, Alice, raise, (*Ra* for *r*) raises, race, races, recess, recesses, rise; arise, (*Er* for *r*) arises, arouse, arouses, erase, erases, ears, oars, errs, airs, miss, misses, muss, aims, noise, annoys, noises, nose, niece, nice, ounce, ounces, woes, woos, yeas, hose, haze, hiss, hisses, house, houses, hews, hues, Hughes, hies, Hayes, pushes, bushes, tushes (upward stem, *Sha*, for *sh* following *Te*, *De*, *Ef*, *La*, *Ra*, and *Hah*), dishes, dashes, fishes, lashes, luscious, rushes, hushes, possessed, pacify, passive, passeth, pestle (*p-s-l*), puzzle, poison, obesity, beset, besides, beseech, basks, abusive, bustle (*b-s-l*), baser, besom, business, basin, baseness, absence, upset, tasty, outside, task, tassel, teasel, desk, dusk, dusky, dusty, decides, decisive, diseased, docile (either upward or downard *l*), desire, desirous, disrobe, dislike, dispels, disloyal, dozen, Chesapeake, chosen, chisel, Jason, jostle, cusp, cask, cassock, excessive, chasm, cosmos, cousin, Casino, castle (*k-s-l*), Castile (*k-s-t-l*), gasp, gossip, gusto, guzzle, fiasco, fizzle (*El* stem), fosil, vessel, vassal, visage, thistle (*El* stem), lisp, receive (*r-s-v*), misty, mask, listen (*El* stem), lessen, lesson, loosen, reason, risen, rosin, resume remiss, missile, muzzle, music, musk, mosque, mistletoe (*m-z-l*), mouser (*Ra* stem), miser, misery, honesty, nasty, necessity, necessary, nestle, nozzle, insist, resist, subsist, desist, system, scissors, saucer, season, Susan, schism, Sicily, successive, unsafe, unseen, Owasco, anxiety, anxious (*Ing-Ish-ls*), hasty, hastily, husk, hassock, husky, hustle (*La* stem), hasten, Hosannah, hussar (*Ra* stem).

SHORT SENTENCES.

Miss Dewey's roses. Laura's peaches. Olive's mosses. Leave Johnny's books. Naughty Darius Howe chews gum. Katie loves nice, rich coffee. Miss Lillie Snow ate savory soup. Choose right ways. Resist laziness. Lizzie eats ripe, juicy pears. Maurice's slow coach. Sadie's ice houses. Newell Dyer's sons rise early. Viola passes Jennie's house. Sadie supposes wrongs. Lucy loves Johnny. Susan rose sad. Lizzie sings Katie's merry song. Johnny's cows eat husks. Dogs chase cows. Mollie hates snow. Chicago's chime-bells ring merry music. Tommy's owl eats mice. Honesty satisfies reason. Boys leap slow. Lena loves rainy days. Seek happiness.

LESSON VIII.

LOOPS FOR *ST* AND *STR*.

1. A small loop written initially on stems expresses *initial st* sounds; written finally, expresses *final st* or *zd* sounds. Illustration: *step*, *state*, *steak*, *still*, *star*, *starry*, *stem*, *stony*, *past* or *passed*, *guest* or *guessed*, *mist* or *missed*, *honest*, *abused*, *gazed*, *aroused*, *housed*. See lines 1-3 below.

2. A large final loop on stems expresses *str*. Illustration: *pastor*, *toaster*, *faster*, *Lester*, *yester*. See line 4 below.

3. A circle is written on the back of loops to express *s* or *z* following *st* or *str*. Illustration: *posts*, *posters*. See line 5 below.

4. The loops can be used in the *middle* of words provided, at the point of junction, the stems do not cross each other. If the stems cross, the loop is reduced to the value of the *s* circle. Illustration: *destiny*, *testify*, *yesterday*. See line 6 below.

5.—READING EXERCISE
ON ST AND STR LOOP.

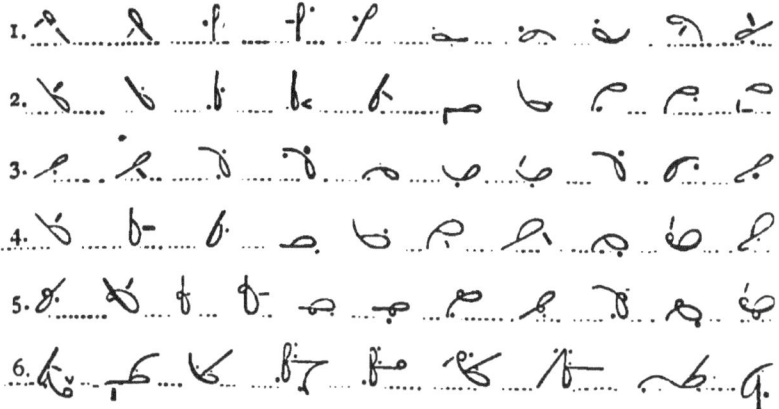

6.—WRITING EXERCISE
ON ST AND STR LOOPS.

Steep, step, stop, stoop, stab, stub, state, stout, steady, study, stitch, stage, steak, stake, stick, stack, stalk, stock, stuck, stucco, stag, stiff, stuff, staff, stave, stove, Stacy, steal, steel, stale, stall, stole, stool, still, stilly, Stella, style, steer, star, store, starry, story, steam, stem, stony, sting, stung.

Pieced, paste, paced, pest, pester, past, passed, posts, posters, beasts, baste, boasts, boaster, boost, bust, busts, abased, abused, teased, taste, toast, toaster, tests, attest, dost, dust, dusters, adduced, doused, chaste, chased, chests, Chester's, jests, joist, cased, kissed, cast, castor, coast, coaster, costs, Custer's, gazed, guests, guessed, ghosts, aghast, feasts, faced, fist, fast, faster, fussed, Foster, vest, vast, vaster, least, laced, list, lest, Lester's, last, luster, loosed, erased, erst, arrest, aroused, raced, roast, roaster, wrist, roused, roosts, roosters, mists, missed, masts, masters, amassed, amused, most, mast, musters, nests, Nast, honest, Nestor, songster, songsters, waste, waists, West, Wistar, Worcester (Wooster), yeast, yester.

Artist (*Ra* for *r*), artists, reduced, richest, rejoiced, refused, revised, upraised, ballast, tallest, utmost, teamster, dullest, coolest, calmest, mildest, forests, forester, fensed, evinced, announced, renounced, artistic, statistics.

SHORT SENTENCES.

Air-castles fade. Hester despises wrong. Step fast. Lester eats roast lamb Tuesday. Despise laziness. Invest safely James Post chased Chester West. Jack's master testifies.

SEMICIRCLES AND HOOK.

LESSON IX.

BRIEF SIGNS FOR *WA* AND *YA*.

SEMICIRCLES.

Wĕ, *Wŭ,* *Yĕ,* *Yŭ.*

1. Small semicircles for *w* and *y* are employed in a large class of words, adding greatly to legibility, and facilitating ease and speed of writing. Illustration:

weep, web, waits, watch, walks, yacht, yokes, unyoke, yellow.

2. The small circle is conveniently written within *Wĕ* and *Wŭ* signs to express *sw* in certain words. Illustration:

sweep, sweet, swig, swings, suavity.

WA HOOK ON LA, RA, EM, UN.

3. Brief *Wa* is joined to *La, Ra, Em,* and *Un,* as a hook. Illustration: *wail, wore, wem, wen.* See next page, lines 6-7.

4. The circle for initial *s* is written on the *Wa* hook of *Ra,* but never on the hooks of *La, Em,* and *Un*—the circle and *Wa* stem being used for *sw* preceding these three stems. Illustration: *swore, swells.* See next page, line 8.

YI, YOI, YOW.

5. The trifthongs *yi, yoi, yow,* are expressed by brief *Ya* joined to the difthong signs. Illustration:

genii, Honeoye, meow.

NOTE (*a*).—In joining *Wŭ* to *Pe, Be, Ka, Ga,* and *Ing,* observe that the motions of the pen are similar to those made in forming a plain figure 2.

(*b*).—In joining *Wĕ* to *Te, De, Cha, Ja,* and *Ish,* observe that the motions of the pen are like those made in forming a figure 9, while *Yĕ* is joined to *Te, De,* and *Ith,* by a motion similar to that in forming a figure 7.

6.—READING EXERCISE
ON BRIEF WA AND YA SIGNS.

7.—WRITING EXERCISE
ON BRIEF WA AND YA SIGNS.

Wipe, web, Webster, witty, wittily, wet, wettest, wait, witticism, weeds, wade, wades, widows, widest, witch, bewitch, watch, wage, wedge, weak, wake, walk, woke, wicks, wax, waxes, waxed, wigs, wife, waif, woof, weave, weaves, wives, withe, wash, wing, wings.

Sweep, swop, swoop, swab, sweet, sweeter, sweetest, sweetly, sweat, Swede, swayed, switch, swig, suave, suavity, swath, swathe, swash, swing, swung, assuage, assuages, unswayed, unswathe, Zouave.

Weal, wail, wall, wallow, wool, wooly, Wallace, Willis, Wells, willow, welcome, wellfare, wealth, unwell, unwieldy, unwelcome, wealthy, Willoughby, war, wore, weary, wary, worry, wear, ware, wares, beware, worse, worst, worth, worthless, worthy, unworthy, warm, worm, wormwood, swore, swear, swears, soirée, swarm, swarms, swarthy, wammel, wem, wean, wane, win, wins, winnow, wen, wan, won, wanes, wince, winces, winced, windy, window.

Yacht, yoke, unyoke, yak, youth, youths, Uriah, Yulee, Yale, yell, yellow, yellowish, (upward stem for *sh*), yawl, yelp, yelk, yore, (*Ar* stem), yarrow, (*Ra* stem), yam, yon, yawn yawns, Eunice, uinique, unity, unite, young, youngster, yank.

Genii, Honeoye, meow.

SHORT SENTENCES.

Willie Wallace works. Willie Woods sings sweetly. Eunice buys cheap cake. Young Yulee's yacht. Johnnie's young sheep. Fannie's kitty "meows," Wednesday. Yellow dogs wag yellow tails. Wet dogs yelp. Jennie sweeps. Emma eats sweet cookies. Wage war young swells, unworthy youths. Willie's bees swarm warm windy wet days. Swing young wives sweetly. Dissuade Webster's unwelcome youngster. Welcome wealth worthy youths.

LESSON X.

BRIEF *WA* AND *YA* SIGNS DISJOINED.

1. The semicircles for the coalescents, *W(oo) Y(ē)* cannot be conveniently joined between stems or at the end of stems, in a large class of words—especially words containing the *y(ē)* element—and are, therefore, disjoined and written in the vowel places, taking the order of vowel sounds and made *heavy* when in the place of *long* vowels and *light* when in the place of *short* ones.

2. Tabular view of brief *Wa* and *Ya* in vowel places:

WA SERIES.

	Long.				Short.	
ᴄ we	in	week	ᴄ wi	in	wit
ᴄ wa	"	wake	ᴄ we	"	wet
ᴄ wa	"	waft	ᴄ wa	"	wag
ᴐ wa	in	wall	ᴐ wo	in	wot
ᴐ wo	"	woke	ᴐ wu	"	wun
ᴐ woo	"	wooed	ᴐ woo	"	wool

YA SERIES.

	Long.				Short.	
ᴗ ye	in	year	ᴗ yi	in	yit
ᴗ ya	"	yale	ᴗ ye	"	yet
ᴗ ya	"	yard	ᴗ ya	"	yak
ᴖ ya	in	yawn	ᴖ yo	in	yon
ᴖ yo	"	yoke	ᴖ yu	"	young
ᴖ yoo	"	you	ᴖ yoo	"	Yucatan

NOTE (*a*).—The *w* signs are made from a circle cut in two vertically, thus: ⊕ while for the *y* signs it is cut in two horizontally, thus: ⊖

(*b*).—The *w* sign in dot vowel places opens to the *right*, or towards the *east*, while the *w* sign in dash vowel places opens to the *left* or towards the *west;* and the *y* sign in dot vowel places opens *upward*, or towards the *north*, while the *y* sign in dash vowel places, opens *downward*, or towards the *south*.

NOTE (*c*).—Observe that the vowel sound in *Wĕ* and *Yĕ* is that of a *dot vowel*, hence *Wĕ* and *Yĕ* are the signs used in the *dot-vowel* places.

(*d*).—The vowel sound in *Wŭ* and *Yŭ* is that of a *dash vowel*, hence *Wŭ* and *Yŭ* are used in *dash-vowel* places.

W AND Y EQUIVALENTS.

3. Before giving a list of words illustrating the use of the disjoined semicircles, it will be an advantage to the student to understand clearly the alfabetic equivalents of *w* and *y*.

The sound represented by *w* is the same as *u* in *quick* and nearly the same as *oo* in *coo* (being briefer in pronunciation than *oo*, and in some words more like *oo* in *foot*), and the final element of the difthongs *o, ow, ew*,—as will be easily perceived by the slow pronunciation of *o*=*o-oo, ow*=*ah-oo, ew*=*e-oo*.

4. The sounds represented by *y* in *you* and *pity* are the same as *e* in *be* and *ĭ* in *it;* but, when followed by another vowel sound in such words as beaut*eous*, op*i*ate, etc., the *e* becomes shorter and the *ĭ* sharper, producing a short sound like unaccented *e* in the syllable *be* in behold. *Y-a, e-a,* and *i-a; y-o, e-o,* and *ĭ-o*, when quickly pronounced, are one and the same thing. For example, the syllable *io* in *folio*, can be spelt three ways—*folio, foleo, folyo*—and indicate the same pronunciation.

5. The following words contain *w(oo)* and *y(ĕ)* sounds represented in different ways by alfabetic equivalents, without changing the pronunciation: Iowa=Io-ooa=Ioa; Owen=Oooen=Oen; bowie=bo-ooy=bo-I; boa=bo-ooa=bowa; bivouac=bivooac=bivwac, quick=kooik=kwik; twig=tooig=tuig; sweet=sooeet=sueet; Yale=ĕale=ĭale=; yank=ĕănk=ĭănk; India=Indea=Indya; opiate=opeāte=opyate ; atheist=athī-ist=athyist; carrier=carre-er=carry-er; anterior=antereor=antery-or.

6. There are a few words in which the syllabication might seem changed by the use of a sign that suggested the letter *y*—such as ‿ *barrier*, ‿ *merrier*, the fonografic forms of which suggest the spelling of the words with a *y* and *two r's*, instead of *three*, thus: *meryer, baryer*, and syllabized thus, *mer-yer, bar-yer*, instead of thus, *mery-er, bary-er;* but as there are no such words as *mer-yer* and *bar-yer*, no confusion can arise by the use of the *y* sign. The words *collier (yer), lawyer*, etc., would never be pronounced *colly-er, lawy-er*, for the reason that there are no such words in the language. English speaking students will have no difficulty in distinguishing between these two classes of words.

7. There are a few concurrent vowels—the initial one of which is accented—which better be expressed by their separate signs, thus:

idea,   pean,   séance,   eon,   eolis,   Leo,   Leon,

writing nearest to the stem that vowel which is heard *next* to the stem.

8. The concurrent vowels in such words as *bowie, boa, doughy, Owen,* etc., are more conveniently and quickly expressed by the dash for *o* and a brief *w* sign joined, than by the exact vowel signs written separately—taking advantage of the terminal *oo* or *w* element of *o*, and representing it by the brief *w* sign, which sign carries with it, or, at least, suggests on account of its names, *Wĕ* and *Wŭ*, an accompanying short vowel sound, dot or dash, according to the direction in which it opens. Illustration: ⸺ *bowie,* ⸺ *doughy,* ⸺ or ⸺ *Owen,* ⸺ *oasis*—using *Wĕ*, because it represents *w* with a *dot* vowel sound following it. ⸺ *boa,* ⸺ *Noah*—using *Wŭ*, because it represents *w* with a *dash* vowel sound following it—the vowel sounds in these words being invariably pronounced in ordinary speech (even by the best scholars), nearer like the vowel in *up* than like short *ah*. By taking advantage of this pronunciation a distinction can be made between ⸺ *boa,* and ⸺ *bowie* ⸺ *Noe* and ⸺ *Noah,* etc., etc.

NOTE.—While it may seem teaching a tautophonical pronunciation to represent the vanish or terminal sound of *o* by both the *o* dash and brief *w* sign attached to the *o* dash, it is necessary to so represent it in order to secure a sign that will *join* legibly to the dash and at the same time represent, or suggest, the short vowel sound following the *o* sound. The student may regard that the dash represents the radical or initial sound of *o* (short, as in *whole*), while the *w* sign represents *both* the vanish or terminal sound of *o* and the short vowel following it; or he may, if preferred, regard the dash as representing full *o*, and brief *w* sign as representing only the short vowel following. Either way, it expresses the same thing.

9. The concurrent vowels of *poet, poem, bowie, boa, towage, Zoe, Noe,* if expressed by their separate signs, are written thus:

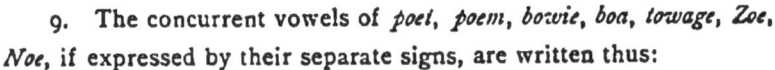

but if by their joined signs, thus:

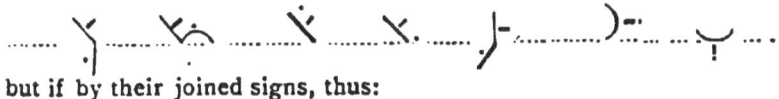

It will be seen that the joined signs are more readily and quickly made, for the following reasons: The student does not have to think of the particular place by the side of the consonant stem in which to write the sign of the *second* vowel, and does not have to lose time in pen-liftings or in going back to place the vowel to a downward stem, as in the words *poet, towage,* etc. Besides, it enables the vowels to be read in their proper order, forward or downward, instead of backward or upward, as in the words *bowie, towage,* etc., where the separate signs are written.

10. The concurrent vowels in *deity, deist,* etc., can be quickly and legibly expressed by a *single* sign, thus: |ᵛ *deity,* ꞵ *deist,* ꞇ *theist,* etc., instead of thus: |⋯ ꞵ⋯ etc.

11. Concurrent vowels having any other than *e, i, y, oo, o, w,* for the initial vowel must be expressed by separate signs, thus: ˙ᵛ *payee.*): *Isaiah,* (:⫯ or (·⫯ *laity,* ⫯⫯ or ⫯⫯ *gayety,* ⁓ *rawish.*

12.—READING EXERCISE

ON BRIEF WA AND YA DISJOINED.

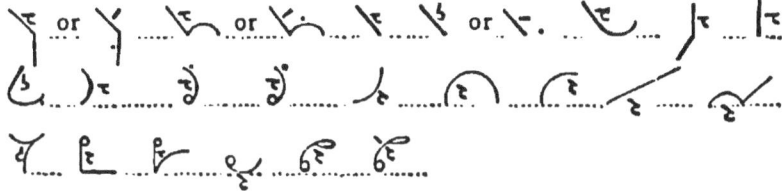

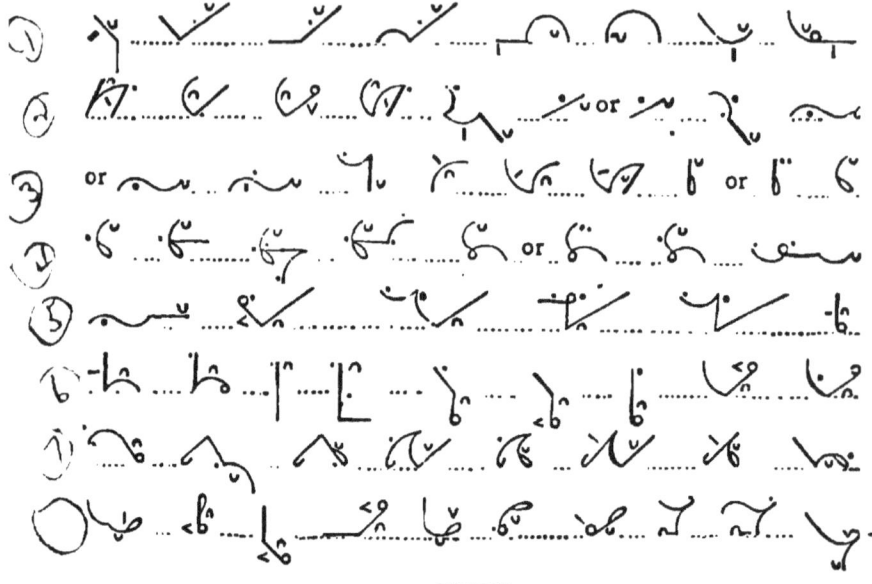

13.—WRITING EXERCISE

ON BRIEF WA AND YA DISJOINED.

Poets, poetic, poem, bowie-knife, boa, towage, doughy, Zoe, showy, Louis (Lool), lower, Louisa, rower, mower, Noe, Noel, Noah, hoer, oasis, oases, stoic, Stowell, snowy, slowest, soloist.

Opiate, barrier, carrier, merrier, Collier, lawyer, piano, fiasco, geology, theology, theory, theories, theorize, theorized, Zenobia, Zenia, area, Arabia, mania, ammonia, India, olio, folio, folios, foliage, deist, deistic, theist, atheist, atheistic, atheistical, atheistically, atheism, insignia, maniac, superior, exterior, inferior, interior, anterior, odious, odium, idiom, idiot, idiocy, idiotic, piteous, beauteous, tedious, copious, copiously, furious, various, impious, happier, happiest, wealthier, wealthiest, worthier, worthiest, balmiest, funniest, studious, studiously, dubious, curious, tinier, tiniest, sorriest, silliest, annual, manual, biennial.

Payee, pean, idea, gayety. séance, Isaiah, laity, Leo, Leon, eolis, rawish, eon.

ASPIRATE TICK, HEH.

LESSON XI.

HEH ON STEMS.

1. A small inclined tick for initial *h*, is used on the following stems: *Em*, *Er*, and *Wa*. Illustration:

home, *homely*, *harm*, *whistle*.

2. *Heh* is also used on the joined brief *w* signs and hook, made in the direction of *Pe* or *Cha*, and written upward or downward according to convenience of joining. Ilustration:

whip, *wheat*, *whack*, *whiff*, *whale*, *whir*, *whine*, *whim*.

3.—READING EXERCISE
ON ASPIRATE TICK.

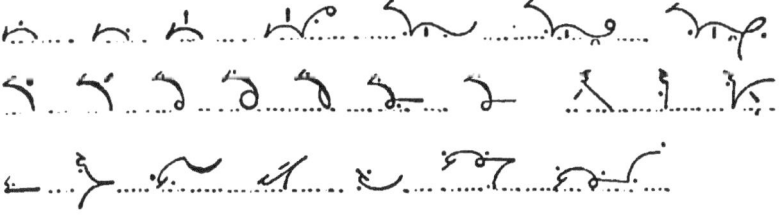

4.—WRITING EXERCISE
ON ASPIRATE TICK.

Hymn, hem, ham, hum, hemal, Hummel, homely, homeliness, homeless, homelike, homicide, homo, homily, hominy, humility. hammock, harm, harmless, harmony, harmonize.

Whey, whoa, whiz, whizzes, whist, whittle, Whittlesey, whistle, whistler, whisk, whiskey, whiskers.

Whip, Whipple, whop, whopper, wheat, Whateley, Whitelaw, whittle, Whitcher, whack, whacks, whig, whiff, whang.

Whale, whaler, Wheeling, whir, whirs, whirl, whirligig, wharl, wherry, wharf, wharves, whim, whimsical, whine, whinney.

ABBREVIATIONS AND POSITION.

LESSON XII.

ABBREVIATIONS.

1. There are certain words of common, frequent use, that, for the sake of greater speed in writing, are abbreviated in their fonografic representation, the same as words are abbreviated in common print; that is, expressed by one, two, or more of their letters or signs, instead of all. About two-thirds of these abbreviations are complete in their *consonant* representation—the *vowels* only being omitted; and although the advanced fonografer never writes the vowels in any word, except when absolutely necessary, these *special* words—with vowels, only, omitted—are placed in the list of abbreviations, because they are *never* to be vowelized but learned as the special, fixed signs for those words; while the words not in the list of abbreviations are vowelized or not, as the writer finds necessary.

2. Some words are abbreviated by omitting the consonants, retaining only the vowel, while other words, still, are represented by brief signs such as the circle, loops, half-circles, etc.

VOWEL RULE OF POSITION.

3. Before giving a list of abbreviations it will be necessary to explain what is termed "The vowel rule of position." It is already well understood that there are *three* PLACES by the side of a consonant stem for vowels. Corresponding to these three *vowel* PLACES are three *stem* or *outline* POSITIONS governed by the vowels: Words containing a *first place* vowel to be written in *first position—above* the line; words containing a *second place* vowel to be written in *second position—on* the line; words containing a *third place* vowel to be written in *third position—thru* or *under* the line.

4. The *first* position for *upright* and *inclined* stems is HALF the height of a *Te* stem above the line; and for horizontals and brief signs, about HALF-WAY BETWEEN the lines of writing, according to the vidth between the lines—writing a little below the centre on widened paper.

5. The *second* position for *all* signs is on the line of writing.

6. The *third* position for *upright* and *inclined* stems is THROUGH ι ACROSS, the line; and for horizontals and brief signs, UNDER the line.

7. It is a great aid to legibility to write, not only the greater number of abbreviations, but also words of ONE SYLLABLE in the *position* indicated by the vowel—or accented vowel, if a word contain more than one.

8. Some of the abbreviations are not written according to the "vowel rule of position."

(*a*).—This occurs where there are two or more words having the same outline and containing vowels of the same class; they require to be written in different positions to prevent conflict and confusion, as well as hesitancy in reading. See signs for *do* and *had, each* and *which, if* and *for*, etc.

(*b*).—Again, where there is but *one* word of a certain stem or outline, it is always written in second position, regardless of the vowel rule, because that position is the most natural, and favors ease and speed of writing. See sign for *your*.

(*c*).—Where there are two words of the same outline and vowel class, the most frequently-occurring one is given the second position. See signs for *each* and *which*, *ease* and *was*, *law* and *will*, *are* and *our*, *no* and *own*.

(*d*).—Where there are two words of the same outline, but differing vowels, the most frequently occurring one takes the second position, regardless of the vowel, and the other one the next position to it. See *which* and *much*, *think* and *thank*.

9.—SIMPLE STEMS.—NO. 1.

ARRANGED ACCORDING TO THE FONOGRAFIC ALFABET.

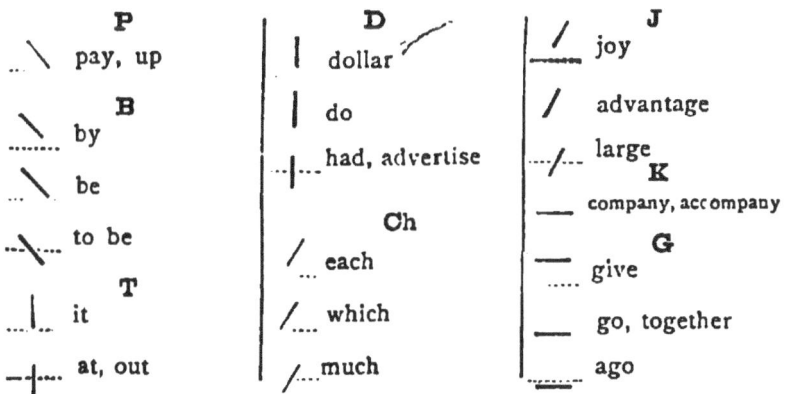

	F		Z		N
⸺	if, off	)	ease, easy	⌣	in, any
⸺	for	)	was	⌣	know, no
⸺	few		Sh	⌣	own
	V	⌣	she, wish		Ng
⸺	ever	⌐	shall, shalt	⌣	thing
⸺	have	⌐	issue	⌣	long, along
⸺	view		L	⌣	language
	Th	⌐	law		W
(	think	⌐	will	⟍	why
(	thank-ed, thousand	⌐	allow	⟍	way
	Dh		R	⟍	away
(	thee, thy	⟍	year		
(	they, them	⟍	are		Y
(	tho', thou	⟍	our	⌐	your
	S		M		H
)	see	⌒	me, my	⌐	high
)	say, so, saw	⌒	may, am	⌐	Ohio
)	us				

10. Final *s* is added to any of the above signs by writing the circle on the end of the stem.

11.—SHORT SENTENCES.

Pay up your bills. It will be your dollar each time they go. It was in my wish. Which way will they go? Why do they ask them for it? It was years ago. They know why it was so. Do they ever go up? Have they ever thanked? They say so. It will be easy for us. Shall they go away? They will wish them much joy. Each company will be large. Do they see any advantage in it? It was to be so. They may think so. If they do, she shall know it. Does she own it? No, she knows it. They had it out each day. Your things are in Ohio.

12.—COMPOUND STEMS.—No. 2.

peculiar-ly-ity			familiar-ly-ity
publish-ed			especially
belong			like
become			look
to become			alike
talk			lawyer
take			irregular-ly-ity
took			argue
dignity			refer
acknowledge			regular-ly-ity
catholic			represent
kill			make
came, come			many, money
effect			among
affect			into
fact			unto
forever			notwithstanding
follow			enjoy

⁀	knowledge	⌣	anything
⁀	enlarge	⌒ or ⌒	nothing
⌒	never	⁀	N. Y.
⋌	nevertheless	⌒	N. H.
⁀ or ⌒	only	⋀	half
⌒	newer	⋀	hope
⌣	name	⋀	happy

NOTE.—Should the student think these abbreviations difficult to learn, let him notice that very few of them are abbreviated beyond the omission of vowels, so that once looking at them is sufficient to learn them. Those that are abbreviated by the omission of consonants should be written over several times, and then, by practising them in short sentences they will be remembered.

13.—SHORT SENTENCES.

Notwithstanding many peculiar things, they are happy. Nevertheless, anything will do for them Hope for many things. Never follow lawyers. Do nothing half-way. Enjoy knowledge forever. Enlarge your knowledge. Never follow peculiar ways. They came in time for your lawyer's money.

LESSON XIII.

ABBREVIATIONS—Continued.
I.—CIRCLES, LOOPS, AND VOWELS.—No. 3.

	is, his			themselves
	as, has			says
	first			size
	subject			as well as
	subjected			sir
	best			ours, hours
	its			seem
	said			same, some
	such			something
	just			seen
	suggest			soon
	because			necessary
	signature			most, must
	several			stenographer
	these, thyself			honest
	this			next
	thus, those			wise

......).......... west		....6........... uses, uzes	
......: 6........... yes, yours, yourself		...... 6....... used	
.... 6....... use, uze		.........9..... yesterday	
------ 6̸......... usage		.... highest	

2. The affix "self" is expressed by a *small* final circle on stems, and "selves" by a *large* circle.

3.—WRITING EXERCISE

This is peculiar. They will enjoy themselves. This subject was used yesterday. Will they suggest something? She is a first-rate stenographer. Several said it was so. Yes, they go West next Wednesday. She is as happy as they are. The boy says his things will come as soon as they wish for them. They have only necessary things. She used yours several times yesterday. They are honest as well as wise. His highest aim is to be just. Be just, because it is best. His signature is necessary, as well as yours.

4.—VOWEL SIGNS.—Nó. 4.

...... the	\...two, too	..\...to
_ . a, an	.l...owe, oh, O!	..l....but
......and	/....who-m	.../....should
........all	....of	 I
......awe	......or	..,..how
.... ought. aught	.....on, he, him	..6..whose

5.—READING EXERCISE.

6.—WRITING EXERCISE.

The boy has a dog. I see a duck and an owl. They are all up stairs. At sight of it I was in awe. He ought to go soon. Too many of them are in the house. It is too much for him to do. Who took my book? To whom will he go for counsel? He or I must see to it. Will they talk to him? He will go, but I shall stay. Should he think best, they may have it. How soon will he come? Whose book is this? How long have they had it?

LESSON XIV.

ABBREVIATIONS—Continued.

1.—BRIEF WA AND YA SIGNS.—No. 5.

we	what	yet
with	would	beyond
were	ye	you

2.—VOWEL, STEM, AND BRIEF SIGN COMBINATIONS.—No. 6.

idea	area
now	while
knew, new	well
I'll, I will	where
I'm, I am	aware
already	whereas, worse
altogether	wherever
together	wheresoever
almighty	when
although	one
almost	whence
whoever	once
however	whenever
	whensoever

.... whencesoever   .... withdraw
.... without   .... withal
.... within   .... you're, you are

3.—READING EXERCISE.

4.—WRITING EXERCISE.

It is now time we were on our way. What would you do for him? When and where would it be best to go? Which one is it? What is the area of the State in which you live? I hope she is no worse. He may go without it altogether. We are within two miles of the house. Your ideas will have weight. Do you know yet how it is? How long ago was it? Whenever you are right go ahead. I am aware of the fact. Whoever he is we must see him.

HALF-LENGTHS AND ED TICK.

LESSON XV.

HALVING STEMS TO ADD *T* OR *D*

1. A stem can be halved to add the sound of *t* or *d* at the end of words or syllables. Illustration:

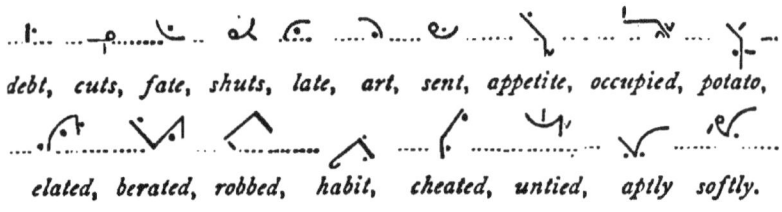

debt, cuts, fate, shuts, late, art, sent, appetite, occupied, potato, elated, berated, robbed, habit, cheated, untied, aptly softly.

SHADING THE UNMATED HALF-LENGTHS.

2. When the stems *La, Er, Em*, and *Un*, are halved to add *d* let them be shaded; but when halved to add *t* let them remain light. Illustration:

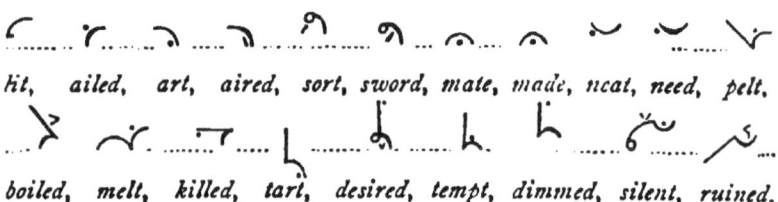

hit, ailed, art, aired, sort, sword, mate, made, neat, need, pelt, boiled, melt, killed, tart, desired, tempt, dimmed, silent, ruined.

3. The half-length stem for *lt* is written according to the same rules as full-length *La*, while the half-length for *ld* is invariably made downward, because it is *shaded*, and is vowelized the same as *Ya*—from the top down, because it is made downward, like *Ya*. Illustration:

delight, polite, knelt, lead, lad, puzzled, spoiled, mailed, nailed, revealed,

NOTE.—The vowel after a halved stem at the end of such words as *rated, righted, elated, avoided*, etc., is understood to be *ĕ*, therefore it is never necessary to write it.

ED TICK.

4. The syllable *ed* at the end of such derivativ words as *fated, sifted, remitted*, etc., where the primativ word *fate, sift*, etc., is halved to add a final *t* or *d*, is expressed by a small tick, written in the direction of *Te* or *Ka*, at the end of a word. Illustration:

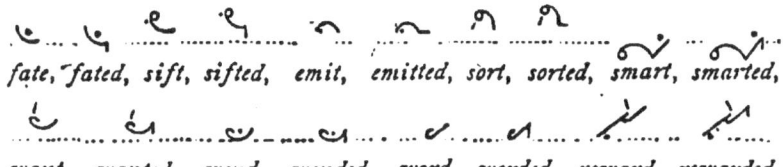

fate, fated, sift, sifted, emit, emitted, sort, sorted, smart, smarted, want, wanted, wend, wended, word, worded, reward, rewarded.

5. The *ed* tick is also used at the end of full-length stems where it is not convenient or advisable to add the *d* sound by halving. Illustration:

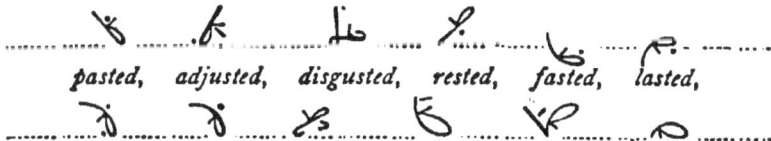

resisted, exhausted, imitated, animated, stated, studied.

6. The *ed* tick is written after the loops. When following the *str* loop it expresses only *d* with the vowel *e* omitted- Illustration:

pasted, adjusted, disgusted, rested, fasted, lasted,

arrested, wasted, hoisted, fostered, bolstered, mastered.

7. The halving principle is very sparingly used in writing straight-stem words of *one* syllable; such words as *peat, pit, beat, bought, boat, bead, coat, cud, goat, guide*, etc., being written by the majority of reporters with both stems, while others use the halving principle and never omit the vowels. Illustration:

or   or   or   or

peat,   beat,   bought,   coat.

8. For convenience in speaking or writing, the halved stems can be named by adding the *t* or *d* sound to the stem name. Example: Pe, Pet or Ped, etc.; Ef, Eft; Ve, Vet or Ved; Ith, Itht; The,

Thět or Thěd; Es, Est, etc.; La, Lăt or Lăd; El, Eld; Er, Ert or Erd; Ra, Răt or Răd; Em, Emt or Emd; Un, Unt or Und; Hah, Haht or Hahd. This will make distinguishihg terms for *p*, *t*, etc., expressed by *stems*, and *p*, *t*, etc., expressed by *halving*.

9. *Ing*, *Wa*, and *Ya* are never halved.

10. The circle or loop on halved stems always read last. Illustration:

pets, sifts, salts, sorts, meets, needs, midst, didst, couldst.

11. The reporter writes *st* loop on halved stems to form the superlative degree of certain adjectives. Illustration:

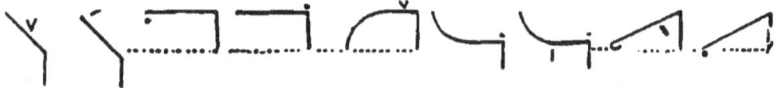

late, latest, soft, softest, neat, neatest, smart, smartest.

WHEN NOT TO HALVE.

12. The halving principle does not apply in the following cases:

(*a*). When initial *Ra*, in words of one syllable, is followed by *t* or *d*—writing such words as *right, rite, rate, road, rood, ride*, etc., with stems for *t* and *d*.

(*b*). When a final vowel follows *t* or *d*—writing *pity, tidy, duty, fatty, veto, muddy, naughty, lady*, etc., with stems for *t* and *d*, in order to furnish places for the vowels following the *t* and *d*.

(*c*). When the consonant before the *t* or *d* is both preceded and followed by vowels—writing such words as *abate, abode, acute, avoid, allayed, amid, unite; parried, borrowed, torrid, carried, furrowed, varied, married, narrowed, harrowed, pallid, tallowed, dallied, gullied, followed, valid, mellowed, inlaid (La* for *l), wallowed (Wa* hook*), hallowed, yellowed* (brief *Ya*), etc., with stems for *t* and *d*.

(*d*). When concurrent vowels come before the *t* or *d*—writing *poet, diet, fiat, laureate, naid*, etc., with stems for *t* and *d*.

(*e*). When *t* or *d* follows a stem preceded by another stem, with which it does not form an angle. Ilustration:

piped, bobbed, kicked, gagged, liked, fact, faggot, harrowed, reared.

OF PHONOGRAPHY. 51

13.—READING EXERCISE.

TERMINAL HALF-LENGTHS.

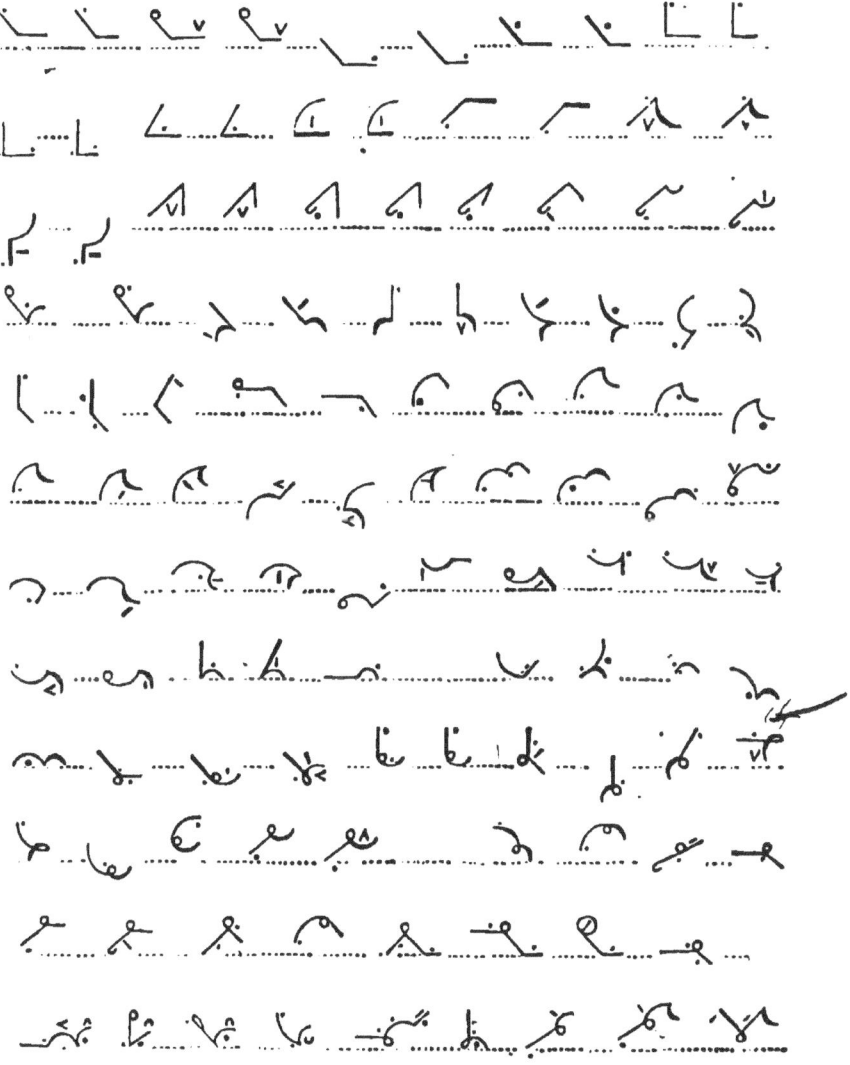

INITIAL HALF-LENGTHS.

TWO HALF-LENGTHS.

ED TICK ON HALF-LENGTHS.

UPWARD ED TICK.

14. In writing the *ed* tick on *Lāt* it is better to strike it upward, on account of the liability, in rapid writing, of the downward tick becoming a hook. Illustration:

wilt, wilted, salted, related, emulated, diluted.

DISJOINED WHOLE AND HALF-LENGTHS.

instituted, substituted, destitute, pathetic, emphatic, synthetic.

15.—WRITING EXERCISE.

Pick, picked, poke, poked, pack, packed, tick, ticked, tuck, tucked, tack, tacked, checked, joked, jagged, reasoned, limit, remit, limited, remitted, elect, elected, erect, erected, sift, sifted, scent, scented, sound, sounded, rescind, rescinded, resound, resounded, descend, descended, decent, descent, dissent, dissented, absent, absented, invite, invited, indict, indicted, repeated, reputed, inhabited, uninhabited, remedied, innocent

16.—ABBREVIATIONS—HALF-LENGTHS.—No. 7.

put	issued	afterward
bad	let	forward
about	lead	inward
did	old, world	outward
debt	lord, read	better
doubt	might	debtor
caught	immediate-ly	yield
could	made	until
act	not	little
God, got	under, hand, hundred	write
get, good	sent, cent,	written
thought	want, wind	writing
that	went wont	retain
east	wild	astonish-ed
wished	word	establish-ed

17.—READING EXERCISE.

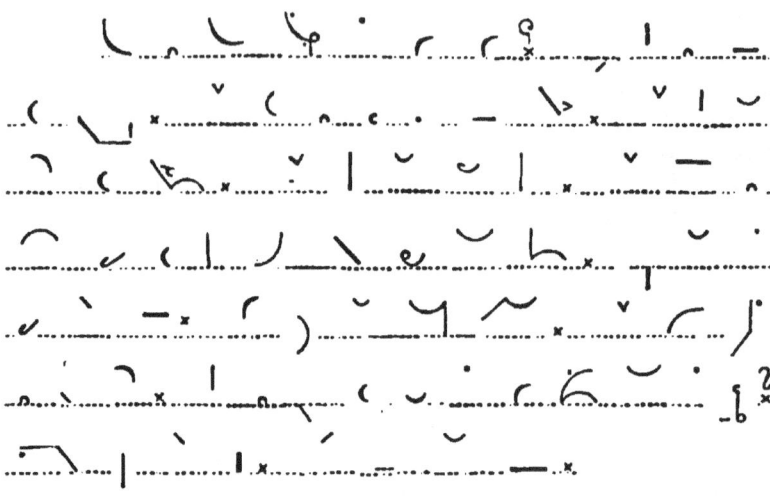

18.—WRITING EXERCISE.

You would enjoy a visit to the old world. I want you to give me your word that you will do all the good that lies in your power. Never go in debt. Read only good books. The Lord God leadeth me. We went to the woods afterward. Do not be too forward. That was a good act. He could not read for the want of a book. He is not a bad boy. Put your cap on the rack. How much good and beauty we have in this world! Have you any doubt about it?

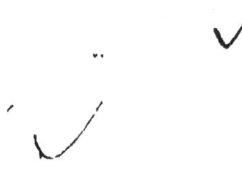

INITIAL HOOKS.

LESSON XVI.

SMALL INITIAL HOOKS FOR L AND R, ON MATED STEMS.

1. When either *l* or *r* immediately follows any other consonant they are expressed by a small hook at the *beginning* of the consonant stem. Ilustration:

pl,	bl,	tl,	dl,	chl,	jl,	kl,	gl.
pr,	br,	tr,	dr,	chr,	jr,	kr,	gr.
fl.	fr,	thl,	thr,	shl,	shr.		

2. In writing the hooks on stems, the first motion of the pen is made in an opposite, parallel direction to the stem; and the next and last motion is at right angles with the stem, as shown in the accompanying illustration:

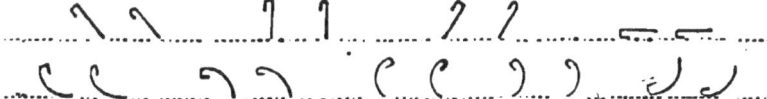

Let these characters be practised with care until the hooks can be readily and perfectly made. Careless writers incline to make these hooks look like loops or circles. It is just as easy to make them right as wrong, if proper care is exercised in the beginning to understand the principles of movement in forming them.

L HOOK WORDS.

3. Notice that the *l* hooks are on the *right* and *upper* side of the stems.

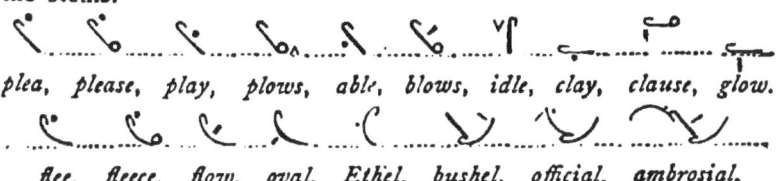

plea, please, play, plows, able, blows, idle, clay, clause, glow. flee, fleece, flow, oval, Ethel, bushel, official, ambrosial.

R HOOK WORDS.

4. Notice that the *r* hooks are on the *left* and *under* side.

pry, praise, brew, breeze, tree, eater, trust, odor, draw, dress,

cry, crow, ochre, acre, grow, ogre, egress, grass,

freeze, frizzes, frost, throw, ether, thrust, usher, azure.

5. In comparing the *l* and *r* hook signs, let the student regard

pl, tl, fl, thl,

and so forth, as so many pieces of wire bent so as to form the initial hook, and that these same pieces of bent wire, when TURNED OVER, become

pr, tr, fr, thr.

To illustrate still more clearly, let them be written in pairs, as follows:

etc.,

pl, pr, bl, br,

fl, fr, vl, vr, thl, thr, dhl, dhr, shl, shr, zhl, zhr,

—the *shr* and *zhr* forms being *turned over endwise* to give the forms for *shl* and *zhl*.

SPECIAL VOWELIZATION.

6. The initial hooks are intended for the expression of *l* and *r* preceded by a stem consonant without a vowel between the stem and

hook consonants, as in *play, pry,* etc., and for the expression of such syllables as *ple, ble, fle, per, ber, ter,* etc., in *couple, bible, trifle, reaper, fiber, cater,* etc.; but there are many words of long, awkward form, such as *collect, correct, fulcrum, telegram,* etc., that are shortened in outline and rendered even more legible by using these hook signs; and for this class of words special rules, for showing that the vowel is to be read *between* the hook and the stem, are given.

7. When the vowel heard belongs to the *dash* class, represent it by the dash sign struck through the stem at right angles—made *heavy* for *long* vowels and *light* for *short* ones—and written in first, second, or third place, the same as in ordinary vowelization. Illustration:

fall, cold, full, fulcrum.

8. As the shape of the dots will not admit of their being written through the stem and be distinguished, like the dashes, the vowels of the *dot* class are represented by small circles, written, for *long* vowels, *before* upright and inclined stems, and *above* horizontal ones; written, for *short* vowels, *after* upright and inclined stems, and *below* horizontal ones, observing, as usual, the three vowel places. Illustration:

feel, fail, carpets, fill, fell, paroxysm.

9. When the vowels heard in *err* and *air* are to be read between the hook and stem, indicate it by making the parallel dash signs into ellipses, thus:

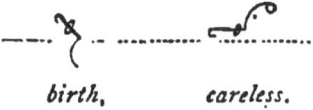

birth, careless.

10. The difthong signs are either struck *through* the stem, or else written at the beginning or at the end of stems, to denote that they are to be read *between* an initial hook and stem, thus:

cure, casual.

II.—READING EXERCISE.

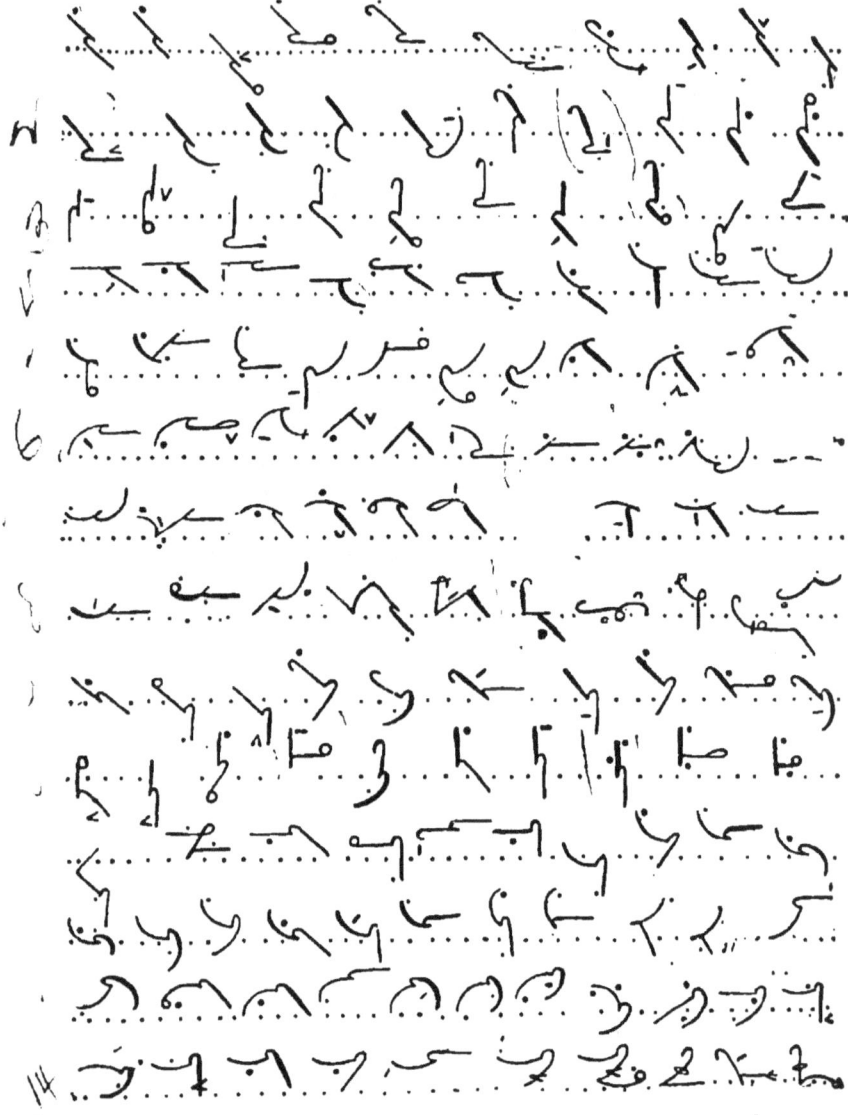

12.—WRITING EXERCISE.

Apple, able, clue, eclat, please, pleases, pleased, play, played, plow, blow, blaze, blazed, idle, idles, clay, close, glaze, glass, fly, flow, fleece, flees, flies, flows, fleeced, oval.

People, peopled, pickled, buckled, tickled, cockled, giggled, fickle, cobble, gable, table, stable, stubble, scuffle, faithful, truthful, mouthful, treacle, draggle, prattle, brittle, scuttle, fiddle, victuals, thickly, flatter, blacker, flavor, pressure, special, initial, nuptial, impartial, impartiality, social, prudential, especial, ambrosial, casual, visual, official, officially, bleach, oblige, club, cloth, clothes, clash, claim, gloom, youthful, vocal, unable, muddle, employ, simple, sample, example, dissemble, resemble, tumble, rumble, devil, level, lawful, ankle, uncle, angle, ethical, plaster, blister, bluster, cluster, cloister.

Pray, pry, brow, tree, trio, eater, try, utter, tray, draws, odor, cry, crew, acre, agree, free, fray, offer, offered affray, threw, throw, author, usher, azure.

Price, prize, prizes, prized, breeze, braced, trace, trust, trusted, crust, crazed, grist, grazed, grazes, grasses, thrice, thrust, precise, process, blazes, crisis, crises.

Prop, problem, prime, probe, approach, preach, pretty, bribe, brick, brag, brush, bravo, broom, broil, brier, briny, bridge, breeches, breath, breathe, break, bring, trip, tribe, trick, track, truth, trim, trash, drug, dream, droll, drear, dreary, drouth, dressy, creep, crape, group, grim, grab, growl, grog, frog, freak, frail, thrill, throng.

Paper, pauper, taper, dipper, cheaper, jobber, keeper, caper, copper, gutter, figure, vigor, vapor, vicar, entry, sentry, pitcher, major, lodger, ledger, archer, richer, Rogers, degree, decreed, degrade, sugar (*Sha*), shiver (*Sha*), measure, leisure, erasure, fisher, treazure, treasury, pleasure.

VOWELS HEARD BETWEEN HOOK AND STEM.

Germ, firm, Germany, person, charm, form, George, courage, fulsome, procure, cheerful.

L AND R HOOK ON UNMATED STEMS.

13. The initial hook for *l* on *Em*, *Un*, *Ra*, and *Hah* is made large. Illustration:

ml,   *nl*,   *rl*,   *hl*.

14. The hook for *r* on *Em*, *Un*, *Hah* is made *small*, and the stem *shaded*, to distinguish the *mr*, *nr*, and *hr* combination signs from *wm*, *wn*, and *Hah*. Illustration:

mr,   *nr*,   *hr*.

15. A large initial hook on *La* expresses the other liquid consonant, *r*. Let it be noticed of the two liquids that *La* takes a large hook for *r* and that *Ra* takes a large hook for *l*. Illustration:

lr,   *rl*.

16. The initial hooks for *l* and *r* are never used on *Es*, *Ze*, *Er*, *Ing*, or *Wa*. *Ing*, when hooked initially, being required to express *nr*; and *Es*, *Ze*, *Er*, *Wa*, when hooked initially, being required to express *Thr*, *Dhr*, *Fer*, *Ver*. *Yāl*—*Ya* with initial hook—is not used for anything, as it is an inconvenient form to join; besides, it is quicker and better to express *yl* by the *brief Ya* sign and *l* stem.

17.—READING EXERCISE.

camel, animal, canal, kernel and colonel, spiral, exhale, help, color

rumor, tremor, moral, minor, north, cohere, adhere, inherit.

18.—WRITING EXERCISE

Enamel, canaille, kernel, colonel, enameled, spirals, relapse, relapsed, relax, relaxes, relaxed, spinal, spaniel, channel, panel, canal, final, flannel, penal, vernal, finally, coral, choral, floral, rural, barrel, peril, Tyrol, thoroughly, help, helper, helpless, health.

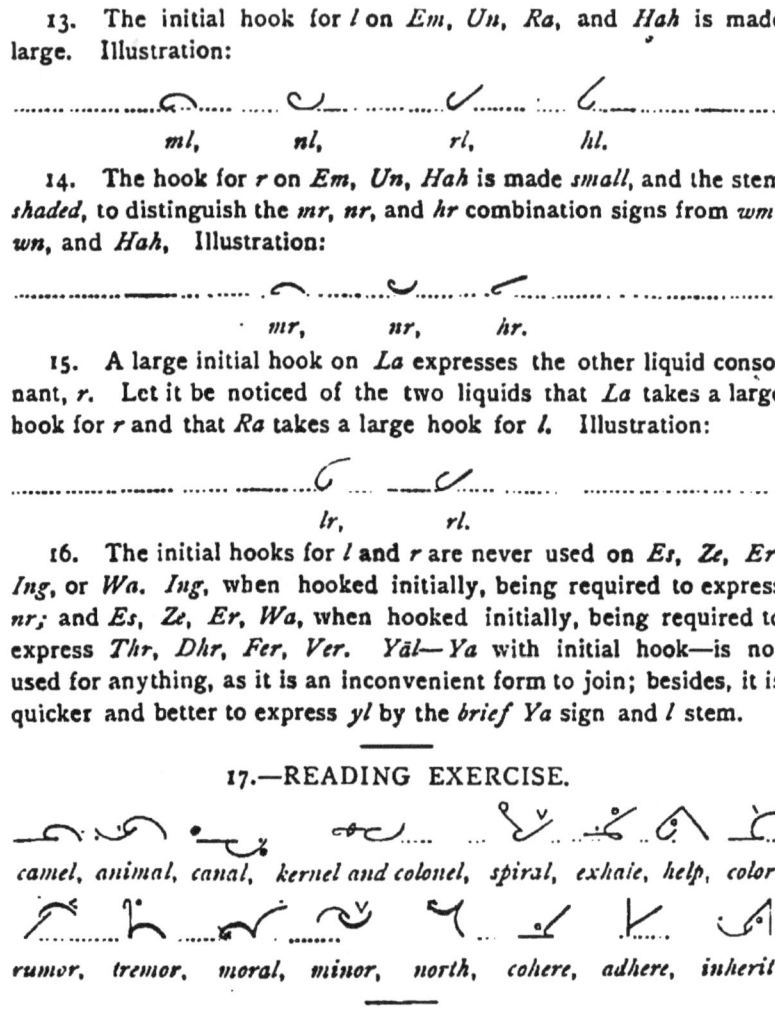

healthy, healthier, healthiest, healthful, heliotrope, halcyon, helm, helmet, inhale, unwholesome, exhale, unhealthy, color, collar, scholar, secular, Fowler, valor, raillery, stickler.

19.—*L* AND *R* HOOK ABBREVIATIONS.—No. 8.

R HOOK, STRAIGHT STEMS.

appear	true	larger
principal-ly, principle	doctor	care, occur
practise	dear	cure, accrue.
re-member	during	correct-ed
number	cheer	aggregate-ed
utter, truth	chair	agree.

L HOOK, STRAIGHT STEMS.

able, ably	deal	call
till, tell	deliver-ed	clerk
at all	children	collect-ed

R HOOK, CURVED STEMS.

form	either	humor
from	there, their	near, nor, honor
over	other	hire
every, very	sure, assure	hear, here, her
aver	share	hair
author, three	Mr., mere	remark
through	more	manner

L HOOK, CURVED STEMS.

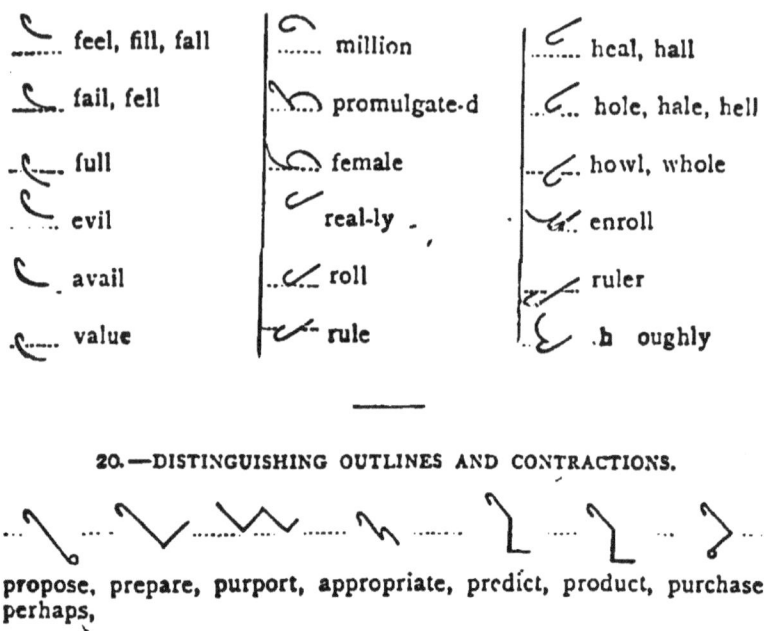

20.—DISTINGUISHING OUTLINES AND CONTRACTIONS.

propose, prepare, purport, appropriate, predict, product, purchase. perhaps,

protect, dark, church, credit, courage, accuracy, girl.

declare, calculate, report, reporter record, regard, important, required, importance.

import-ed, impart-ed, insurance, current, crowned, grant, grand, ground.

LESSON XVII.

THE INITIAL CIRCLE ON *L* AND *R* HOOK SIGNS.

1. To prefix *s* on *r* hook signs, the hook is made into a circle.
2. To prefix *s* on *l* hook signs, the circle is made *within* the hook. Illustration:

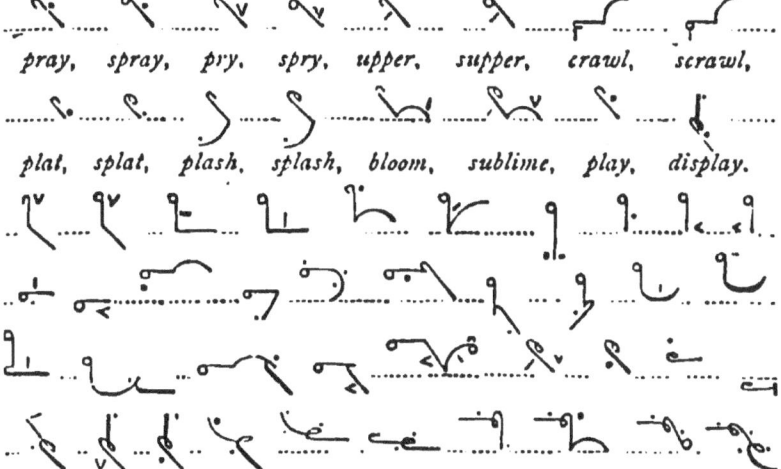

pray, spray, pry, spry, upper, supper, crawl, scrawl,

plat, splat, plash, splash, bloom, sublime, play, display.

3. The circle on *Ka*, before an *l* hook on *Pe* and *Be*, is elongated or flattened, like a loop, and the pen is carried entirely *over the stem* before it turns to form the hook; thus enabling the writer to get that part of the hook, where it joins the stem on which it belongs, quite distinct.* Illustration:

excusable, explored.

4. In writing such words as *disagree, descry, prescribe,* etc., the circle is written on the right side of the first stem, and the second stem, which is *Ka* or *Ga,* is written directly out from the top of the circle. This brings the circle on the *r* hook side of *Ka* and *Ga*. Illustration:

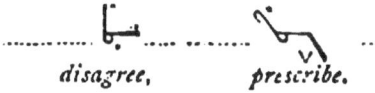

disagree, prescribe.

---

* Some writers make the turn of the pen directly *on* the *Ka* stem, instead of allo the *crossing over*. That way which is easiest and most legible to the writer is the *best*.

5. Many writers omit the *r* representation in the words *describe, prescribe*, etc., and express them thus:

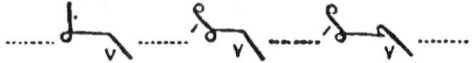

6. In writing the circle on the *r* hook side, *between* stems running in the *same* direction, it is not necessary to show the hook, as the *left* and *under* side of straight stems is known to be the *r hook side*, while the *right* and *upper* side of straight stems is known to be the *circle side*. Illustration:

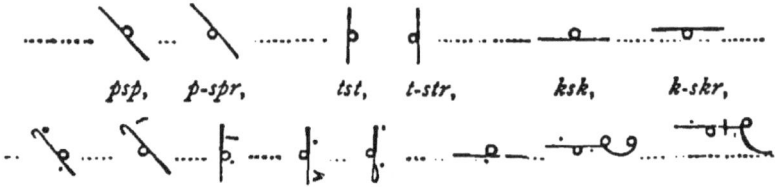

psp, p-spr, tst, t-str, ksk, k-skr,

precept, prosper, dusty, destroy, distressed, cask, excrescence, excursive.

7. *Per* preceded by *Dis* is written thus; as in the words *disappear, disparage, dayspring*, etc.

8. In such words as *tasteful, boastful, trustful*, etc., where the *l* hook sign cannot be made following the *st* loop, the pen *crosses the stem*, thus reducing the loop to simple *s* and enabling the writer to form a perfect hook on the *Ef* stem. This contracts the words to *tas'ful, boas'ful, trus'ful*, etc. Illustration:

tasteful, boastful, trustful, breastplate.

9.—WRITING EXERCISE.

Spray, supper, sober, suitor, strew, cider, suppress, cypress, soberly, screw, scarcely, secrecy, sacred, supply, sable, satchel, sickle, cycle, possible, disciple, display, displayed, accusable, physical, peaceful, passively, plausible, classical, classically, crucible, explore, taxable, graceful (the hook of the *Ef* in *graceful* is implied by the circle at the end of the *Ga* stem being elongated like a loop. If there was no *l* hook to express, the circle would be kept *round*, thus:), disgraceful, prosperous, prosperously, distresses.

disaster, disasters, disastrous, cheese-press, Caspar, excreable, excursive, describe, disagreeable, disagreeably, disappear, disparage, dayspring, pastry, pasture (*Pēs-Cher*), extreme, gastric, mixture (*Em-Kās-Cher*), fixture (*Ef-Kās-Cher*), dishonor—, designer, strainer, streamer.

Straggle, struggle, strapper, supreme, soprano, sobriety, strata, stream, streamed, streamlet, strength, strange, stronger, strangest, strut, street, strait, straight, straighter, sprite, sprout, sprayed, desperate, desperately, desperado. whisper, whispered, distrain, distrained, distract, distracted, distrust, distrusted, trustful, distrustful, mistrust, mistrustful, expressly, describe, descried, prescribe, proscribe, subscribed, ascribed, abstract, extract, extracted, excusable, crucible, taxable, explore, explored, explode, exploded, display, displayed, displays, frustrate, frustrated, hemisphere (hemisfere), gossimer, moral, morally, curse, discourse, discoursed,

atmosphere immoral, mortal, immortal, course, persuade.

10.—ABBREVIATIONS.

CIRCLE ON L AND R HOOK SIGNS.—No. 9.

surprise	separated	supply
surprises	scare	supplied
surprised	secure	skill
spirit	scarce	scale
separate	scarcely	school

LESSON XVIII.

BACK HOOK FOR *IN, EN, UN.*

1. The syllables *in, en* or *un*, preceding the *s* circle on *r* hook signs, are expressed by a small back hook, made so as to bring the circle on the *r* hook side of the stem. Illustration:

inspire, inspired, instruct, insecure, unscrupulous.

2. This hook is also used on *sla, ser, sem.* Illustration:

enslave, unceremonious, unseemly.

3.—WRITING EXERCISE.

Inseparable, inseparably, insuperable, unsuppressed, instructor, unstrung, inscribe, insecurity, insoluble, unsolvable, unsalable, unsullied, insular, insult, insulted, unsolicited, unceremoniously, unseemly, ensample, ensemble (ongsombl).

4.—READING EXERCISE.—Sentences.

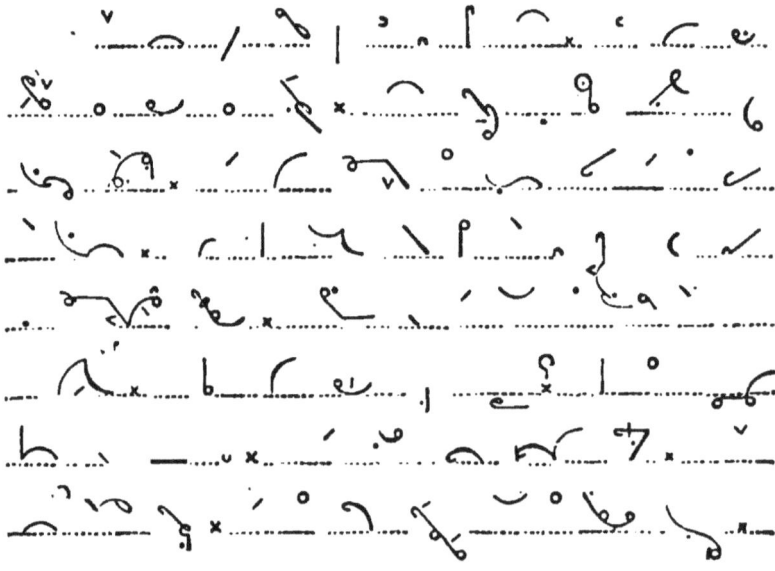

LESSON XIX.

W TICK.

1. The sound of *w* following a stem consonant is expressed by a vertical or horizontal tick joined initially to the stem. Illustration:

twice, dwell, quick, quagmire, thwack, Schwab.

2. Words with an initial *s* and medial *w* sound must be written with the disjoined *Wĕ* or *Wŭ* in its vowel position, thus:

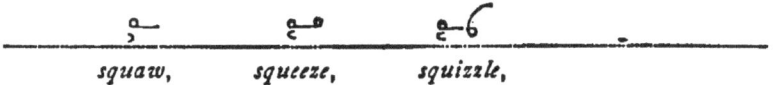

squaw, squeeze, squizzle,

3. Words with *r* immediately following a *w* sound should always be written with the *w*-hook on the *Ra* stem, (*Wĕr*), thus:

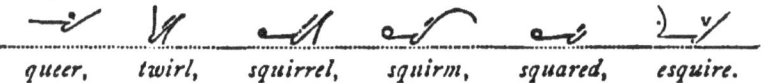

queer, twirl, squirrel, squirm, squared, esquire.

4. *Kwl* words must be written with *Wĕl*, thus:

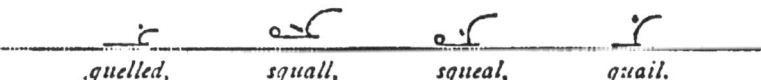

quelled, squall, squeal, quail.

5. The *Wŭ* tick is useful in writing such Spanish names as *Puebla*, *Buena Vista*, etc. Illustration:

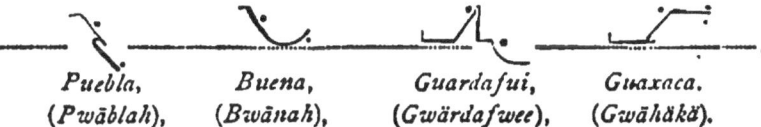

Puebla, Buena, Guardafui, Guaxaca.
(Pwāblah), (Bwānah), (Gwärdafwee), (Gwähäkä).

6.—WRITING EXERCISE.

Words to be written with the *w*-tick: Twist, twists, twisted, untwist, untwists, untwisted, tweezers, twitter, twinkle, twilight, twill, twilled, dwell, dwelt, Dwight, Dwinnell, equip, equipoise, quibble, quiet, quota, quest, bequest, bequeath, quad, quick, quicker, quickest, quickly, quake, quaker, quack, quicksilver, quicksand, quagmire, quaff, quaffed, quoth, quiesce, acquiesce, quasi, quassia.

qualm, qualmish, equator, guano, thwack, thwacked, Thwing Schwarb, Schwartz.

Words in which disjoined *Wĕ* or *Wü* must be used: Squaw, squabble, squatter, squeeze.,

Words in which *Wĭr* must be used. Twirl, dwarf, dwarfed dwarfish, querl, quarrel, quirk, queer, choir, quire, quart, squirt squirted, square, squared, squirm, esquire, query, quarry, quarried, quart, quartette.

Words in which *Wĕl* must be used: Quill, quell, quail, squall sequel, squills, squeal.

LESSON XX.

SMALL TERMINAL HOOKS FOR *N*, *F*, AND *V*.

N HOOK.

1. The sound of *n* at the end of words and syllables, and in the middle of words where no vowel follows it, is represented by a small terminal hook made on the *left*, and *under side*, of straight stems, and on the *inside* of curved stems. Illustration:

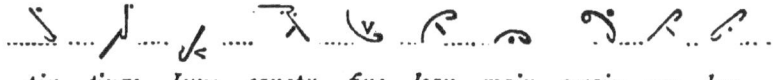

pin, tinge, June, canopy, fine, loan, main, swain, run, hen.

2. *S*, terminating *n*-hook words, is expressed by making the hook into a circle, on straight stems, and by writing a circle *within* the hook of curves. Illustration:

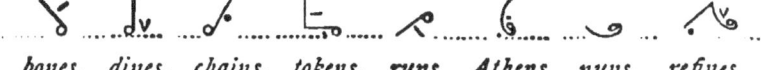

bones, dines, chains, tokens, runs, Athens, nuns, refines

3. The large circle and the loops are written on he *n*-hook side to express *ns-s, nst, nstr.* Illustration:

expenses, enhances, danced, glanced, punster, spinsters.

F AND V HOOK.

4. The sound of *f*, or its cognate, *v*, at the end of words and syllables, and in the middle of words where no vowel follows it, is represesented by a small terminal hook made on the *circle side* of straight stems; and the circle for *s*, terminating *f* and *v*-hook words, is made *within* the hook, to distinguish it from simple *s* without the *f* or *v* sounds. Illustration:

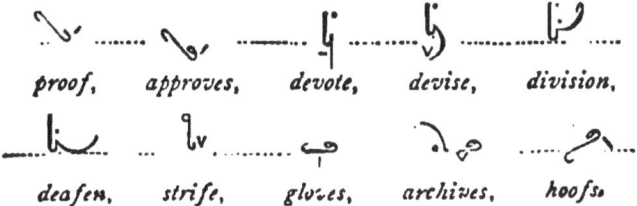

proof, approves, devote, devise, division,

deafen, strife, gloves, archives, hoofs.

5. The hook for *f* and *v* is never written on the curve stems.

NOTE (*a*).—Observe that the *s* circle formed *within* hooks is elongated, like a loop, and made in the direction of the stem to which the hook belongs.

(*b*).—The large circle and the loops for *st* and *str* are never written on hooks.

6. If a vowel follows *n*, *f* or *v*, those consonants must be represented by the *stems*, in order to furnish a place for the vowel. Illustration:

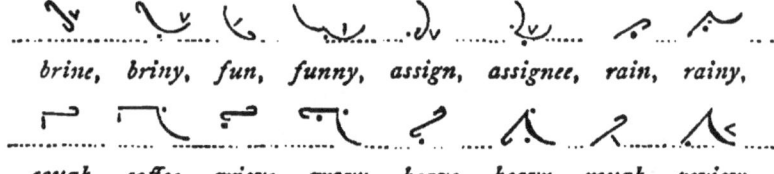

brine, briny, fun, funny, assign, assignee, rain, rainy,

cough, coffee, grieve, gravy, heave, heavy, rough, review.

7.—READING EXERCISE

8.—WRITING EXERCISE.

Pawn, pen, open, bane, bone, tan, eaten, oaten, din, don, chain, chin, June, coin, keen, cane, oaken, gun, gown.

Spun, spoon, sabin, satan, satin, stone, sadden, scan, skin, sicken, sustain, Staten, stewpan, weapon, widen, wooden, waken, wagon, worn, warn, Warren, sweeten, Sweden, sworn, queen, quince, quinces, equinox, equinoctial, equestrian.

Prune, brown, brain, bran, train, drown, drawn, churn, adjourn, crane, acorn, crown, corn, green, grain, grin, groan, twine, twines, twin, twins, twain, entwine, twinge, twinges.

Plain, plan, blown, clean, clan, clown, glean, glen, decline, recline.

Fan, fun, vine, thin, assign, zone, shine, lawn, urn, moon, nun.

Soften, seven, serene, Simon, Stephen, Stamen, flown.

Suspense, strains, screens, widens, stamens, Stevens, woman's.

Puff, bluff, pave, brave, strive, dove, cave, rove.

Puffs, paves, drives, chiefs, Jove's, caves, coughs, cuffs, graves. grieves, gives, roves, raves.

Panic, pancake, pinch, punch, punish, pennon, bandy, banjo, banish, tonnage, Channing, candy, conic, coinage, expunge, experiences, expenses, finish, furnish, vanish, thinness, heathenish, linear, lonely, minute, mInūte, mInūtely, mInūteness, mental, mantel, miner, piquancy, potent, potency, demean, demeanor, vacancy, organic, envenom, phenomena, phenomenon, plenty, planet, plenitude, plunge, blanch, French, fringe, plenary, penurious, penance, finance, synonym, seminary, sponge, Spanish, stauuch, stingy, pippin, bobbin, obtain, barn, Auburn, Italian, deepen, detain, domain, adorn, cabin, roughen, raven, region, regain, famine, foreign, lemon, Lyman, illumine, remain, imagine, machine, engine, tribune, blacken, chairman, African, Mormon, Norman, Herman, Hellman.

Preference, toughen, deafen, deafness, define, divine, devote devout, devotee, devour, reveal, rival, revere, rover, river, revere equivalent, quiver, quaver, hover, beaver, tougher, cover, clever clover, devise, advise, division, devotion, defence, advance, bever age, engraver, provide, provided, provision, Providence, providen-'al, ‿xtravagance, extravagant.

SHORT SENTENCES.

Ten honest men live in one town. Nine fair women spun sixteen skeins of woolen yarn. The moon shines upon the lawn. Green are the banks of Bonny Doon. When it rains, the Robins say, "Cheer up, cheer up, cheer up!" Rover is a brave dog, you will discover, and serves his master faithfully. The Bluff river divides our farm. Never swerve from right behavior. See the rainbow! The poor, with industry, are happier than the rich, in idleness. Put down your pen and join the children in their fun.

9.—ABBREVIATIONS.—*N*, *F*, AND *V* HOOKS.—No. 10.

N HOOK.

opinion	then	begun
upon	than	began
been	alone, loan	turn, torn
done	men	sudden
down	man	at length
join	human	delinquent
general-ly	women	happen
can	woman	punish-ed
gone	known, none	explain-ed
gain, again	union	question
often, phonography	learn	christian
even	pecuniary	correspond
thine	begin	consequential

OF PHONOGRAPHY. 73

	signify-ied-cant		southern		prudential
	western		pertain		prominent
	fallen		appertain		permanent

HALF-LENGTHS.

	point, appoint		consequent		account
	behind, bind		second		annoint-ed
	tend		superintend		round
	attend		acquaint-ed		surround
	did not, didn't		gained		around
	do not, don't		find		understand
	had not, hadn't		found		turned
	gentlemen		foundation		accident
	gentleman		land		subsequent
	kind		mind		returned
	can't		minds		learnt
	cannot		meant, mend, amount		impend

ENS, ENSES, ENST.

	at once		balanced		against
	consequence		occurrence		indispensable
	balance		Kansas		experience
	balances		gains		transcript

F AND V HOOK.

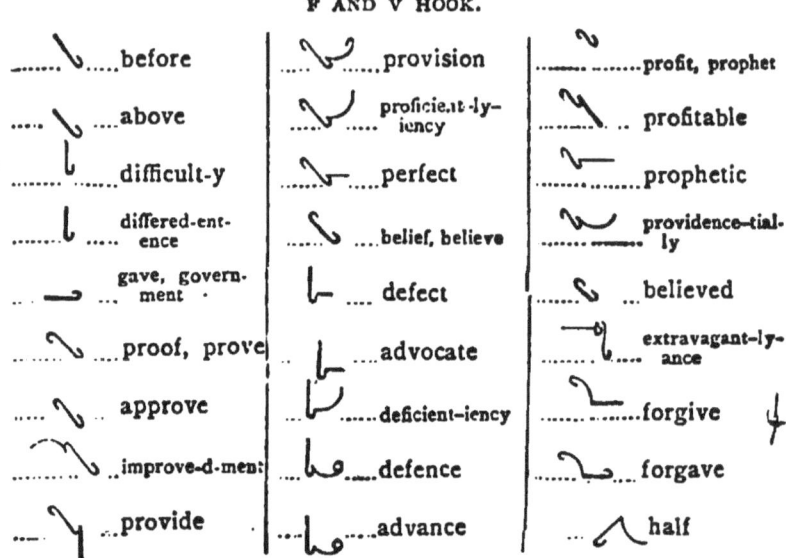

EXPRESSION OF NUMBERS.

1.—Numbers are expressed by the usual Arabic figures: but in writing single figures, 1 and 6, on account of their resemblance to fonografic characters, must be written thus: ⌣ one, ⌒⌢ six.

2.—In expressing but one denomination of numbers, such as millions, thousands, or hundreds, the fonografic signs are used thus: 16 ⌒ 16,000,000; 12 (or 12 ⌢ 12,000; 9 ⌣

LESSON XXI.

SHUN AND *ESHUN* HOOKS.

SHUN HOOK.

1. The syllable *shun* (or *zhun*) following a *stem* consonant, is expressed by a large final hook made on *either* side of straight stems, and on the *concave* side of curve stems. Illustration:

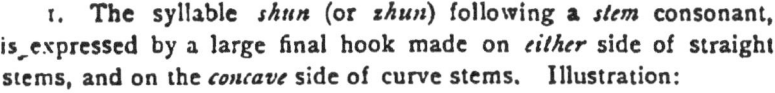

potion, passion, inception, addition, perdition, occasion, sections,

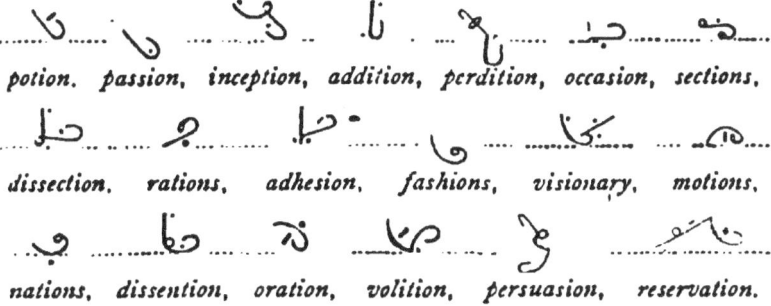

dissection, rations, adhesion, fashions, visionary, motions,

nations, dissention, oration, volition, persuasion, reservation.

2. In writing the words *unction, sanction, distinction,* etc., the stem for the *Ka* sound can be omitted, without impairing legibility. Illustration:

unction, sanctions, distinction.

3. The syllable *ist*, following *Shun* and *Eshun*, is expressed by half-length *Es* (*Est*) on the hooks. Illustration:

elocutionist, factionist, annexationist.

ESHUN HOOK.

4. The syllable *shun* following *s* represented by a *circle*, and a vowel, is expressed by a small hook on the back of the circle. Illustration:

position, decision, accession, physician, cessation, pulsation,

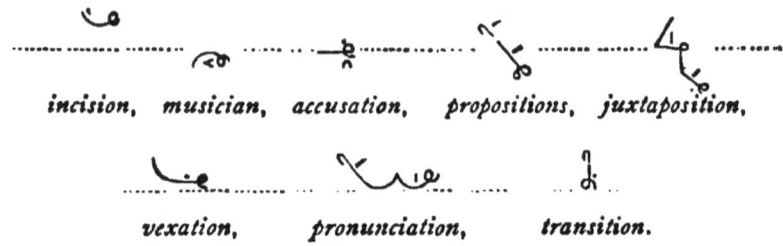

incision, musician, accusation, propositions, juxtaposition,

vexation, pronunciation, transition.

5. Words containing this small hook are legible without writing the vowel that is heard before the hook; but if it is desired to express this vowel any time, write it on the *left* side of the hook for *first place* vowels and on the *right* for *second place* vowels. Illustration:

precision, processions, sensational.

6.—WRITING EXERCISE.

Potion, passion, passions, editions, addition, sedition, section, suction, deception, attraction, attractions, detraction, inception, subtraction, perception, reception, inspection, exception, refraction, infraction, reduction, subtraction, perdition, approbation, attrition, adoration, ration, rations, oration, orations, derision, actions, caution, occasion, fashion, fashions, vision, visions, visionary, cautionary, missionary, nation, nations, national, diction, dictionary, mission, missions, notions, notional, lotion, allusion, solution, adhesion, cohesion, dilation, adoration, admonition, attention, dissension, distention, distraction, restriction, probation, approbation, volition, violation, affiliation, pretension, isolation, recreation, tradition, aggregation, peroration, navigation, apparition, repetition, reputation, selection, election, elocution, elocutionist, elocutionists, factionist, factionists, affectionate, affectionately, observation.

Opposition, position, possessions, decision, causation, accession, accusation, aquisition, physician, physicians, incision, musician, musicians, sensations, proposition, prepositions, supposition, cesssation, secession, annexation, annexationist, pulsations, vowelization, civilization, taxation.

7.—ABBREVIATIONS.—Shun and Eshun Hooks.—No. II.

SHUN HOOKS.

passion	consideration	fashionable-bly
objection	exaggeration	session
objectionable	occasion	association
subjection	creation	missionary
exhibiton	direction	national
tuition	correction	situation
station	collection	dissuasion
instruction	aggression	persuasion

ESHUN HOOK.

opposition	acquisition	conversational
position	procession	conversationist
possession	proposition	compensation
decision	generalization	civilization
accession	organization	realization

SHADING AND LENGTHENING.

LESSON XXII.

SHADING *EM*.

1. *Em* is shaded to express a following *p* or *b*, and is then called *Emp* or *Emb*. Illustration:

imp, stump, hemp, lamp, glimpse, wampum, limbo, embargo.

LENGTHENING *EMP*.

2. *Emp* is lengthened to add a following *r*. Illustration:

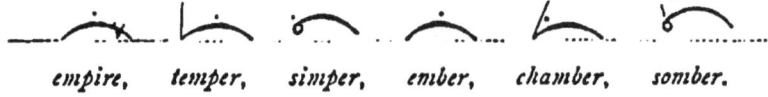

empire, temper, simper, ember, chamber, somber.

3.—WRITING EXERCISE.

Pomp, pumps, bump, damp, dumps, stamp, stump, stampede, jumps, camp, gump, vamp, thump, lamp, lump, limp, romp, rump, mumps, swamp, samp, slump, hump, hemp, primp, plump, tramp, crump, cramp, glimpse, wampum, limbo, Jumbo, humbug, Sambo.

Pumper, Plumper, temper, temporal, distemper, damper, jumper, Kemper, vampire, romper, hamper, scamper, ember, umber, amber, somber, limber, lumber, chamber, slumber, December, November, September, dismember, timber, cumber, encumber, Cumberland, Chamberlain.

LENGTHENING *ING*.

4. *Ing* is lengthened to express a following *kr* (*Ker*) or *gr* (*Ger*). Illustration:

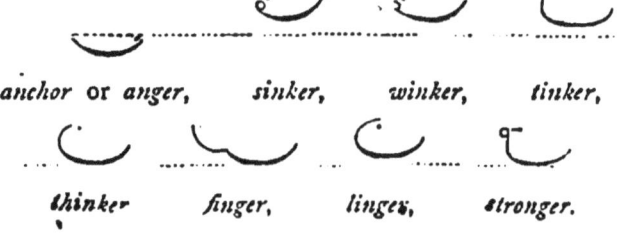

anchor or anger, sinker, winker, tinker,

thinker, finger, linger, stronger.

LENGTHENING THE OTHER CURVES.

5. All the other curved stems are lengthened to express a following *tr, dr, thr, dhr.* Illustration:

enter, render, smatter, mother, philanthropy, father.

6. Of the straight stems, only *Ra* and *Hah* are lengthened to express the following words:

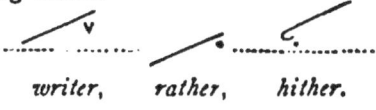

writer, rather, hither.

7.—WRITING EXERCISE.

Anchor, sinker, Bunker, tinker, canker, rancor, ranker, thinker, spanker, winkers, hanker, handkerchief.

Anger, finger, linger, languor, stronger, monger, mongrel, hunger, Hungerford.

Father, fatherless, fatherly, mother, motherly, motherless, thither, nitre, neuter, center, central, Easter, eastern, easterly, Esther, oyster, Astor, Astral, astronomy, astronomical, astronomer, latter, later, literature (*La-ter-Cher*), literary, latterly, literally, collateral, winter, wintered, wander, eccentric, eccentricity, render, hinder, cinder, sunder, wither,   withers, withered   flounder, philantrophy, philanthropist, philanthropical.

Enterprise, interrupt, interruption, entertain, interest, interested, introduce, introduction, interpret, interpretation, interpose, intertwine, interdict, uninterrupted.

8.—ABBREVIATIONS.—Double Lengths.—No 12.

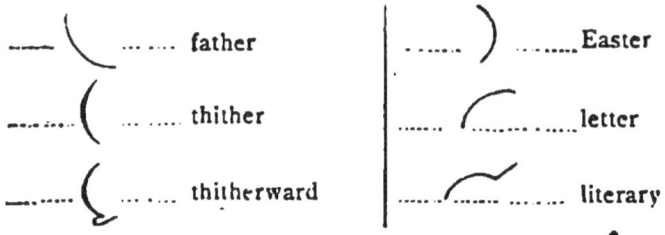

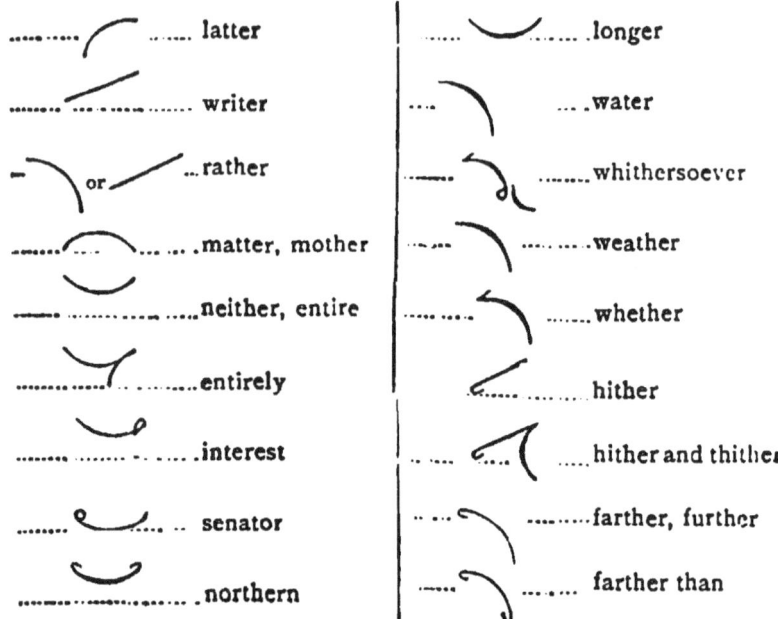

PREFIXES AND AFFIXES.
LESSON XXIII.

PREFIXES.

1.—The prefixes, con, com, cum, cog; contra, contro, counter; fore; magna, magne, magni; circum, self; etc., are represented by brief arbitrary signs written either *before* or *above* the remainder of the word.

CON, COM, CUM, COG.

2.—The sign for *con, com, cum* and *cog* is a *dot.* Illustration:

contain, comprise, cumbersome, cognitiv.

CONTRA, CONTRO, ETC.

3.—The sign for *contra, contro* and *counter* is a *tick.* Illustration:

contradiction, controversy, countermand.

FORE.

4.—The sign for *fore* is *Ef.* Illustration:

forestall, forefathers.

MAGNA, ETC.

5.—The sign for *maga, magne* and *magni* is *Em.* Illustration:

magnanimous, magnetic, magnify.

CIRCUM AND SELF.

6.—The sign, for *circum* and *self* is a small circle. written in *first* position *before* or *above* the remainder of the word, for *circum*, and in *second* position *before* or *above* the remainder of the word for *self.* Illustration:

circumscribe, self-made.

COMPOUND PREFIXES.

7.—Whenever any other syllable comes before these prefixes—thus making a compound prefix—the stem or sign for the syllable is written in the prefix's place, and the prefix is not written, but *implied*, or, *understood* to be expressed, together with the syllable standing in its place; or, in other words, if a stem or circle is written over another stem in such a way as to occupy the place of a prefix sign, it must be read together with the prefix—the syllable that the sign stands for being read first and the prefix last. Illustration:

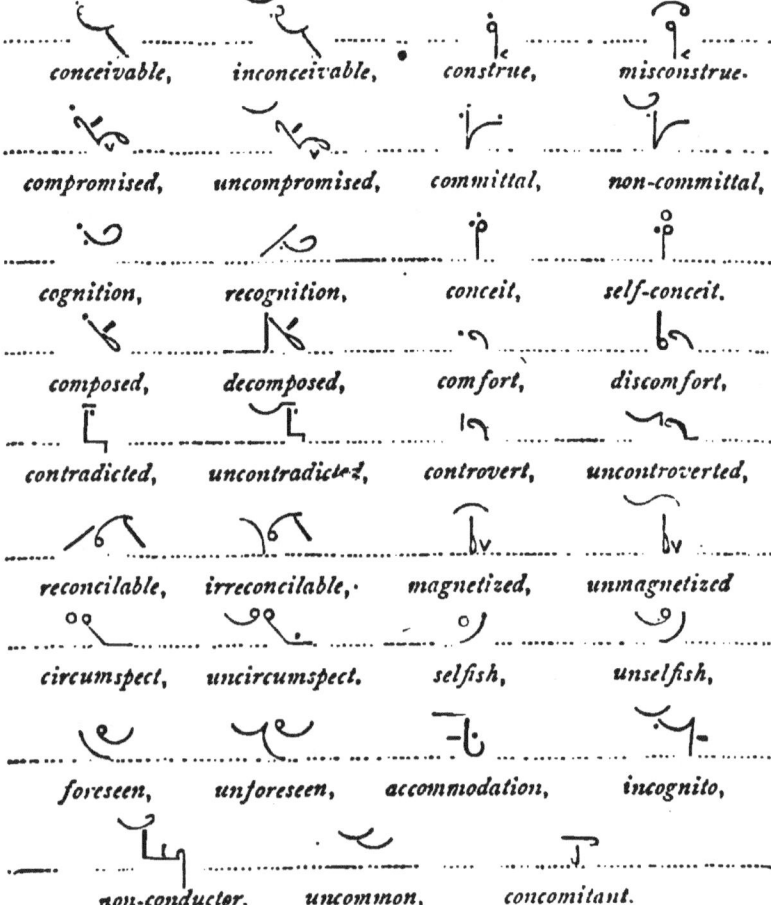

conceivable, inconceivable, construe, misconstrue.
compromised, uncompromised, committal, non-committal,
cognition, recognition, conceit, self-conceit.
composed, decomposed, comfort, discomfort,
contradicted, uncontradicted, controvert, uncontroverted,
reconcilable, irreconcilable, magnetized, unmagnetized
circumspect, uncircumspect. selfish, unselfish,
foreseen, unforeseen, accommodation, incognito,
non-conductor, uncommon, concomitant.

8.—Some words, having the prefix *discon*, are not conveniently written according to the usual rules for writing compound prefix words, in which case, *the remainder of the word* is written *near* the prefix sign, and, in some cases, the prefix is expressed in full, about as quickly as to use a disconnected sign. Illustration:

- *discontinue,*   *discontent,*   *disconnect.*

9.—The syllable *kong*, in *Congress, conquer,* etc., is expressed by the *con* dot, thus:

Congress,   *conquer.*

10.—*Con, com or cog* can be expressed by writing the remainder of the word close to a preceding word, thus:

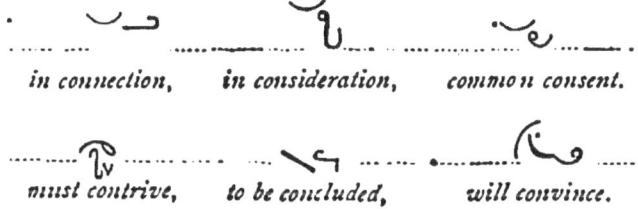

in connection,   *in consideration,*   *common consent.*

must contrive,   *to be concluded,*   *will convince.*

11.—READING EXERCISE.

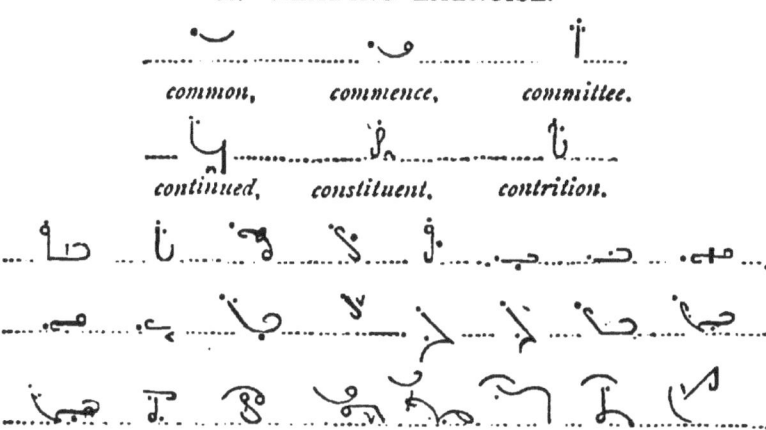

common,   *commence,*   *committee.*

continued,   *constituent,*   *contrition.*

12—WRITING EXERCISE.

Compute, computed, computation, compose, composes, composed, composition, compositor, compost, compound, compounded, compassion, comprise, comprised, compressed, comply, complied, complex, complexion, complication, complicate, combine, contain, contains, contusion, constrain, construction, contrite, contrition, contribute, contribution, consistently, constantly, continue, continued, constrained, condemn, condemnation, conjure, concur, concourse, concrete, conclude, conclusion, conclave, conglomerate, conglomeration, confide, confidence, configuration, conflagration, convex, convivial, convenience, convenient, convey, conveyance, convert, convertible, conceive, conception, completion, compilation, compensation, condense, condensation, contrive, contrives, contrary, conduct, construct, contract, control, controllable, contrasted, console, consolation, consolidate, consolidation, conservatory, conservation, conservatism, concern, common, commune, commence, commenced, conquer, conquerable, congress, congressional, cognate, cognation, cognition, cognomen, cognominal, cognominate.

Accomplish, accomplishments, accommodated.

Inconsistent, inconstant, inconsolable, uncontrollable, unconvinced, unconquerable, inconceivable, uncommon, uncommonly, recompense, recommend, recommendation, recognize, recognizes, recognized, recognition, recognizable, misconstruction, miscompute, non-conformity, non-committal, non-conductor, decomposition, discomfort, disconcert, disconcerted, disconnection.

Contraband, contradict, contradiction, contradistinction, contravene, counterpoise, counterpoint, contrapuntal, counteract, counteracted, counteraction, counter-irritant, counter-irritation, countermand, counter-mine, counter-balance, counterpart, countersign.

Foreknow, fore-ordain, foretell, fore-told, foreknowledge, forewarn, foreseen, foresight, forerunner, forecast, foreshadow, fore-foot, fore-finger, fore-father, foresee, fore-lock, forebode, foreclose, foreclosure, forego, foregone, foreground, forehanded.

Magnanimous, magnanimity, magnify, magnificent, magnitude, magnetism, magnetic, magnesia.

LESSON XXIV.

AFFIXES.

1.—Affixes (also termed suffixes) are expressed by simple stems or arbitrary signs, either joined or disjoined, and are great aids to speed without impairing legibility.

BLE, BLY.

2.—When it is not convenient to write *Bel* (*Be* with *l* hook) for the final syllables *ble* and *bly* the simple stem *Be* is employed Illustration:

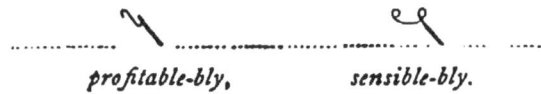

profitable-bly,   *sensible-bly.*

SELF AND SELVES.

3.—When *self* and *selves*, at the end of words, cannot be expressed by their full forms—*Slay-Ef* and *Slay-Ves*—the small joined circle is employed for *self* and the large one for selves. Illustration:

thyself.   *themselves,*

SHIP.

3.—*Ship*, in nearly all cases, at the end of words, is expressed by disjoined *Ish*. Illustration:

friendship,   *partnership,*

LY.

4.—When *La*, for the syllable *ly*, at the end of words, cannot be joined, it is expressed by *La* written *over* or by the *side* of the stem next to it. Illustration:

manly.   *positively.*

ING.

5.—The *added* syllable *ing*, at the end of words, is expressed by a dot directly at the end of the stem or sign. Illustration:

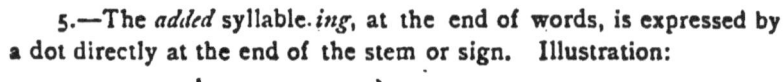

doing,   *saying,*   *owing.*

INGS.

6.—The *added* syllable *ings* is expressed by either a small circle or an inclined tick written in the *ing-dot's* place. Illustration:

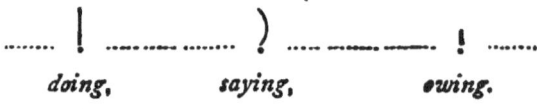

doings,   *sayings.*

INGLY.

7.—The added syllable *ingly*, at the end of words, is expressed by a disjoined *La* written across *ing-dot's* place. Illustration:

knowingly,   *trustingly.*

ABBREVIATIONS AS AFFIXES.

TO

8.—The syllable *to*, at the end of words, following any other stem than *Un*, is expressed by the little vowel sign employed as the abbreviation of the word *to*. Illustration:

thereto,   *hitherto.*

ON.

9.—*On*, at the end of words, is expressed by the *n* hook when it is not convenient to use the regular sign. Illustration:

thereon,   *whereon.*

OF.

10.—*Of*, at the end of words, is expressed by the *f*-hook, on straight stems, but after curves by the little vowel sign employed as the abbreviation for *of*. Illustration:

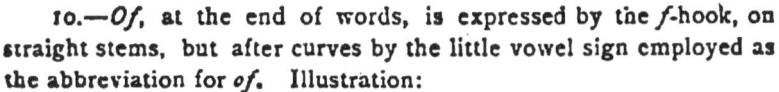

whereof,   hereof,   thereof,

IN.

11.—*In*, at the end of words, is expressed by *Un*. Illustration:

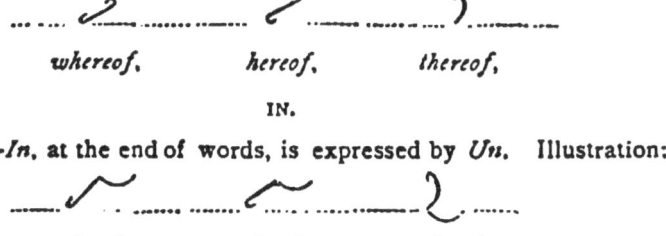

wherein,   herein,   therein.

AFTER AND HAND.

12.—*After* and *hand*, at the end of words expressed by the abbreviations for those words. Illustration:

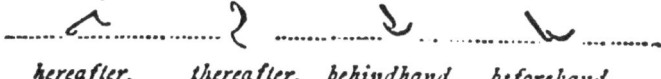

hereafter,   thereafter,   behindhand,   beforehand.

THE CALIGRAPH.

A machine indispensable to students, business and professional men, for legible and rapid writing.

Thousands of them in use.

Can be operated, after a week's use, by young people or men and women as rapidly as longhand writing, and after two or three months's time the speed of writing will increase from sixty to eighty words a minute.

Send for a descriptive circular, price, and list of patrons.

D. L. SCOTT-BROWNE,
23 Clinton Place, New-York, N. Y.

REPORTERS' MATERIAL,

Such as Pens, Pencils, Note-Books, Reporters' Covers, Fountain Pens, Pencil Cases, Pocket Ink-Stands, Caligraphs and Type-Writer Ribbons and Paper, Binder for the MONTHLY, Letter-File, etc., etc., Wholesale and Retail. Send for Price-List.

D. L. SCOTT-BROWNE, *Manufacturer,*
23 Clinton Place, New-York, N. Y.

SCOTT-BROWNE'S COLLEGE OF PHONOGRAPHY.

Principles and Speed imparted. All lessons given by dictation. Pupils advanced by any system desired.

Terms, and Catalogue of about 400 Pupils and Graduates sent upon application.

A thoro course of preparation for business is given by actual dictations in our business and editorial offices, and in doing professional work, as soon as thoro competency has been reached.

The only exclusively Shorthand College in America.

D. L. SCOTT-BROWNE, *Principal,*
23 Clinton Place, New-York, N. Y.

BROWNE'S PHONOGRAPHIC MONTHLY AND REPORTERS' JOURNAL.

Oldest, largest, cheapest, most popular; most shorthand engraving and phonographic news; contributions from every part of the world; leading questions treated editorially. Gives portraits, sketches, and fac-simile notes of eminent reporters; lessons and engraved reading matter for students, by the different leading systems; offered improvements; personal notices of the doings of stenographers everywhere. Unbiased, untrammeled, independent, progressive. Organ of the profession. A specimen copy (free) will convince you that it "is the leading shorthand journal."

Thirty-two royal octavo pages—began publication in 1875. Single number, 20 cts.; year's subscription, $2.00. Grand Holiday Number in December.

D. L. SCOTT-BROWNE, *Conductor and Publisher,*
23 Clinton Place, New-York, N. Y.

ALL ABOUT SHORTHAND AND ITS ACCESSORIES,

with a Catalogue of 400 Pupils and Graduates of SCOTT-BROWNE'S COLLEGE OF PHONOGRAPHY. A 48 page pamphlet of information about books, systems, positions, salaries, Type-Writers and type-writing. Answers all the questions an enquirer would be likely to ask.

For free distribution. Sent to any address for a 3c. stamp.

D. L. SCOTT-BROWNE, *Publisher,*
23 Clinton Place, New-York, N. Y.

www.ingramcontent.com/pod-product-compliance
Lightning Source LLC
Chambersburg PA
CBHW032240080426
42735CB00008B/938